MAY 2 4 2018

# RAF

*The Birth of the World's First Air Force*

Richard Overy

W. W. NORTON & COMPANY
Independent Publishers Since 1923
NEW YORK • LONDON

# RAF

*The Birth of the World's First Air Force*

Richard Overy

W. W. NORTON & COMPANY
Independent Publishers Since 1923
NEW YORK • LONDON

# CONTENTS

# LIST OF ILLUSTRATIONS

# PREFACE

The Royal Air Force was formally activated on 1 April 1918, April Fools' Day. It was an inauspicious date on which to launch the world's first independent air force, and there were hesitations about choosing it. Perhaps the army and the Royal Navy, both for their own reasons wary of the fledgling service, quietly approved the choice of date, hoping that a separate air force would soon prove itself a joke. They certainly both hoped that the RAF and the new Air Ministry it served would not last beyond the end of the war. In this they were soon to be disabused. The RAF survived victory in 1918 and has survived regular calls for its dissolution since, and now celebrates an uninterrupted hundred years.

The birth of the RAF was surrounded by argument and controversy. There already were two air services fighting Britain's aerial contribution to the First World War: the Royal Naval Air Service and the army's Royal Flying Corps. The establishment of an entirely new branch of the armed forces was a political decision, prompted by the German air attacks on London in 1917, not a decision dictated by military necessity. The politicians wanted a force to defend the home front against the novel menace of bombing, amidst fears that the staying power of the population might be strained to breaking point by the raids. From the politicians' viewpoint, the air defence of Great Britain was one of the principal charges on the new force, and it is the defence of the home islands twenty-two years later in the Battle of Britain that is still remembered as the RAF's 'finest hour'. The reality of the past hundred years has been rather different. The RAF has principally served overseas and for most of the century was a force dedicated to bombing and to ground support for the other services. This future was anticipated in the final seven months of combat in 1918 when the RAF, building on the legacy of its two predecessors, contributed substantially to the air support of Allied armies in Western Europe and the Middle East, and organized the Independent Force (independent of the front line) for the long-range bombing of German industrial towns. By the time of the Armistice in November 1918, the shape of RAF doctrine was already in firm outline, even if its future as a separate force was thrown into doubt once the fighting was over.

The birth pangs of the RAF are the subject here. Founding a new service in the midst of a bitterly contested conflict raised all kinds of practical questions which had to be resolved, from the colour of uniforms to the very name itself. The long history of the RAF as an institution was given shape in the earliest days of its existence. There are numerous records to help reconstruct those early days and a wealth of memoir and historical literature to draw on. I am grateful for the help I have received in the archives and libraries I have exploited and for the encouragement of the staff at the RAF Museum at Hendon, where I have been privileged to chair the Research Board. This volume is a small contribution to the wider programme of commemoration in which the museum is engaged. My thanks as ever to my agents, Gill Coleridge and Cara Jones, and to Simon Winder and the team at Penguin, and particular thanks to one of my colleagues on the Research Board, the Head of the Air Historical Branch, Sebastian Cox, for his sound advice on an earlier draft. Needless to say, the views expressed throughout are my own, as are any errors of fact or interpretation that might remain.

Richard Overy,
Exeter and London, 2017

I

# Britain and the War in the Air

A fixed determination to attack and win will be
the surest road to victory.

*RFC Training Manual, 1913*

In 1908, only five years after the Wright brothers' first powered
flight in December 1903, the British novelist H. G. Wells published *The War in the Air*, in which he imagined a near future
when aircraft would decide the outcome of modern war. The
novel's hero, Bert Smallways, watching the destruction of
New York by German airships, reflects on Britain's vulnerability: 'the little island in the silver seas was at the end of its
immunity.'[1] Aircraft changed the whole nature of war. Writing twenty-five years later in his autobiography, Wells noted
with a grim satisfaction that he had written the novel 'before
any practicable flying had occurred', but he had been correct
to predict that aircraft would abolish the traditional divide
between a military front line and the home population, and so
erode the distinction between combatant and civilian. With
the arrival of aircraft, Wells concluded, war was no longer a
'vivid spectacle' for the home front, watched like a cricket or
baseball match, but a horrible reality for ordinary people.[2]
Only seven years separated Wells's novel from the first bombs

to fall on British soil and only ten from the establishment of the Royal Air Force, set up to try to protect Britain's vulnerable people from an air menace described so graphically by Wells at the dawn of the air age.

One of the many remarkable consequences of the coming of powered flight was the speed with which the armies and navies of all the major powers sponsored the development of aircraft –both dirigibles and aeroplanes – for military purposes. The technical development of aircraft in the decade following the Wright brothers was exponential and knowledge of the new invention universal, but for the British people, all but immune to invasion for a millennium, aviation posed a particular strategic threat. This perhaps explains why the evolution of military air power in Britain in the age of the Great War was strongly influenced by public opinion and political pressure and was not solely a result of the military need to respond to innovation. Critics at the time and since have blamed military conservatism for the slow development of organized air power in Britain before 1914 and have assumed that public disquiet, noisily expressed in the popular press, prompted a grudging army and navy to explore the use of aircraft despite harbouring strong prejudices against their use.

The army and navy were, in truth, less narrow-minded than the popular image suggests. The first powered flight in Britain was only made in 1908 by A. V. Roe, who managed a distance of just 60 yards (55 metres). A mere three years later the army began developing a military air arm when the Royal Engineers established an Air Battalion consisting of a company of airships (still considered a major factor for the future of air warfare) and a company of aeroplanes. On 13 April 1912 the King issued a Royal Warrant for a new service, and a month later, on 13 May, the battalion was replaced by the Royal

Flying Corps (RFC), the direct ancestor of the future RAF. The Corps consisted of a military wing, a naval wing, a Central Flying School and a reserve, loosely controlled by an Air Committee with representatives from the two services.[3] A small cluster of soldiers and seamen who had qualified as pilots joined the force. The RFC adopted a modified khaki army uniform and the Latin motto *Per ardua ad astra* ('Through adversity to the stars'), still the motto of today's air force.[4] The intention was to keep a unified corps serving both the army and the Royal Navy, but when Winston Churchill became First Lord of the Admiralty in 1913, he exploited his personal enthusiasm for flight to insist that the navy should have a separate air force.[5] The first commander of the Royal Naval Air Service (RNAS) was Captain Murray Sueter, the director of the Admiralty's Air Department. In July 1914 the RNAS was formally divorced from the RFC just as Europe was about to plunge into war. A year later the Admiralty assumed full responsibility, a bifurcation that was to lead to endless friction between military and naval aviation until united as awkward rivals in the RAF in 1918. In the same month that the RNAS was created, a Military Aeronautics Directorate was established by the War Office to oversee the military wing of the RFC under one of the pioneers of army aviation, Major-General David Henderson.[6]

Both the navy and the army understood that aircraft were likely before long to become assets indispensable to their operations. 'In view of the fact that aircraft will undoubtedly be used in the next war,' wrote the Chief of the Imperial General Staff in 1911, 'we cannot afford to delay . . .' The army Field Service Regulations published in July 1912 were the first to contain reference to the use of aircraft, and in the 1912 field exercises two airships and fourteen aircraft were used for reconnaissance purposes. The observer in one of the aircraft was Major Hugh Trenchard, the man later regarded as the 'father of the RAF'; commander of one of the armies in the exercise was Douglas Haig, who later formed a close working relationship with Trenchard on the Western Front. By the summer of 1914, on the eve of the Great War, a major RFC training exercise saw experiments in night flying, flight at high altitudes, aerial photography, and the first attempt to fit machine-guns to an aircraft. The RFC Training Manual issued the year before stressed the need for offensive aviation well before the means were available.[7]

It was nevertheless true that the RFC was a considerable way behind the development of aviation elsewhere. In France, Austria and Germany rapid progress had been made in military aeronautics; the small Bulgarian air force was responsible for inventing the first modern aerial bomb; and in 1914 the Russian engineer Igor Sikorsky developed the multi-engine *Ilia Muromets* Sikorsky Type V aeroplane, the first modern heavy bomber. British services were slower to respond, partly because they did not anticipate a major European war, partly because public and government were fixated on the battleship arms race, and partly because the British army was so much smaller and less politically powerful than its Continental rivals. When war broke out in August 1914, the RNAS possessed only six airships and ninety-three aeroplanes, many of which were unserviceable, and could field only one flying squadron (the word chosen in 1912 to describe the small air units being formed). The RFC arrived in France with the British Expeditionary Force (BEF) with just four squadrons totalling approximately sixty aircraft. There were 105 officers and 755 other ranks. The French army put twenty-three squadrons in the field, the German army twenty-nine.[8]

The first two years of war provided a steep learning curve for air forces on all sides. Aircraft technology improved all the time, but aircraft remained fragile objects, subject to frequent damage and repair. They were constructed chiefly of wood and fabric, carried a heavy metal engine and were held together with wire or wooden struts. Some idea of the nature of early aviation engineering can be gleaned from the trades assigned to each RFC squadron, which included two blacksmiths, six carpenters, four coppersmiths, twenty-one riggers and four sailmakers.[9] Flying was an exceptionally hazardous undertaking with few base facilities, primitive navigational instruments, and the constant threat posed by sudden changes in the weather. Naval aviators were occasionally sent off over the sea never to be seen again. Diaries kept by servicemen in the RFC talk repeatedly of the cold. Aloft in an open cockpit, thousands of feet up, the temperature was debilitating. The RFC Training Manual in December 1915 listed the clothing pilots and observers were expected to wear to combat the intense cold: two pairs of thick long drawers, a woollen waistcoat, a British 'warm coat' with a waterproof oilskin over it, a cap with ear pads, two balaclavas, a flying helmet, goggles, a warm scarf, and two pairs of socks and gloves.[10]

Although the RFC manuals stressed that aircraft could accomplish little or nothing in 'heavy rain, fog, gales or darkness', pilot records show that flying continued even in cloudy, cold conditions with limited visibility. Advice on weather in the air force Field Service Book was rudimentary: 'Red at sunset . . . Fair weather'; 'Red at dawn . . . Bad weather or wind'; 'Pale yellow at sunset – rain'.[11] Crashes and accidents were as a result routine occurrences. British air forces lost 35,973 aircraft through accident or combat during the war, and suffered the loss of 16,623 airmen, either dead, or severely injured, or prisoners of war. A diary kept by an air mechanic during the later war years gives a vivid description of a typical accidental death:

> Lt. J. A. Miller was taking off in an S.E.5 when he crashed, his machine caught fire & he was burned to death, we were powerless to help him, the ammunition in his guns & boxes was exploding & bullets were flying around, soon the fire died down and his charred remains were taken out of the machine & buried in a wood close by, a wooden cross made out of a propeller marks his grave.[12]

The situation in the first years of the war was not helped by the poor level of training of novice pilots, many of whom would have only twenty hours flying time or less before being posted to operations, where only two hours would be spent learning to fly the frontline aircraft assigned to them. A young John Slessor, later Chief of the Air Staff in 1950, recalled that he was commissioned as an RFC pilot with just twelve hours solo flying, and was fortunate to survive.[13] There were no parachutes.

The RFC and the RNAS were military midgets compared with the other branches of the army and navy, and it was still not entirely clear what aircraft might achieve in the context of a major war. All experience prior to the war suggested that the principal function of aircraft, whether aeroplanes or airships, would be reconnaissance of an enemy's military or naval forces, and for much of the four-year conflict the supply of intelligence became an essential and central function of all air force operations, military and naval. 'The most important role of aeroplanes in war,' according to the 1915 Training Manual, 'is reconnaissance.'[14] Moreover, as one senior RFC officer claimed in 1917, 'Aircraft reconnaissance is the most perfect and the most complete it is possible to obtain in war.'[15] This was true only to an extent, since reconnaissance operations were often interrupted by poor weather, while aircraft could be destroyed by ground fire and hostile planes, or disappear altogether at sea. Reconnaissance involved observation of enemy troop movements and dispositions, but, as trench warfare set in, aircraft were also used to spot enemy artillery and to direct the artillery fire of their own forces. This became an increasingly sophisticated operation as the war went on. Aircrew used either the 'target-battery line', when they could see both the objective of fire and the guns doing the firing, signalling by wireless the number of yards the shells were wide, short or long, or the 'clock code' system, where the observer placed the enemy target at the centre of an imaginary clock face 1,000 yards wide and signalled back the 'time' and distance to the gunners on the ground, who had a map and a clock-face disc to enable them to locate the target with greater precision.[16] On a static front line, with artillery duels a regular feature, directed gunfire became indispensable.

Reconnaissance was nonetheless only one of the functions aircraft were expected to perform. In the first days of war RFC pilots and observers practised using pistols or rifles to attack enemy aircraft engaged in observation. Soon, machine-guns were fitted to most aircraft so that those on reconnaissance could protect themselves from attack. By the end of 1915, RFC manuals classed counter-force operations ('fighting against other aircraft') as a key function, without which other duties could not be carried out. The relentless offensive against the enemy air force became a primary objective as the war continued. The third major task was support of surface forces, whether ships at sea or troops on the ground. For the RFC this involved 'destruction of matériel, and demolition at vulnerable points on the enemy's communications' and 'offensive action against troops on the ground'.[17] Ground support operations were conducted using bombs and machine-guns, but from very early in the wartime career of the RFC it was assumed that the impact on the morale of enemy troops was more important than the physical destruction possible with small 20lb bombs, an assumption that came to be embedded in British air doctrine for a generation.

Independent bombing operations, however, were still not regarded as a significant element in air warfare. The RNAS is generally credited with launching Britain's strategic bombing when, at Churchill's prompting, a handful of naval aircraft attacked the sheds and repair facilities of the German Zeppelin airships. On 22 September 1914 four planes attacked targets in Cologne and Düsseldorf, with little effect; on 8 October, two more attacked and struck a Zeppelin hangar, destroying airship LZIX; on 21 November the Zeppelin factory at Friedrichshafen was attacked by a number of small Avro 504 single-seat aircraft, capable of carrying just four 20lb bombs. It was, Churchill told the House of Commons, 'a fine feat of arms', and indeed it was remarkable that targets were found and attacked so far from the front line, given the limitations of current aviation technology; but the raids were tiny and the impact in the end insignificant.[18] The RNAS continued to plan for independent bombing operations against German military targets. In May 1916, No. 3 Wing was established to undertake long-range bombing more systematically, but the Battle of the Somme that summer forced the diversion of RNAS aircraft into assisting the army. Between October 1916 and April 1917 the wing undertook twelve small raids on targets in Germany, but was then disbanded with little achieved and the aircraft again diverted to the land battle.[19] Where bombing mattered in the first years of war it was against targets at or near the front, but even here its effect was marginal.

As the air services grew rapidly in size in the first two wartime years, new organizational structures had to be created. In November 1914 the RFC was divided into two wings, the First Wing supporting the British First Army, the Second Wing supporting the Second Army. A third headquarters wing was added in April 1915. Each Army had an 'aircraft commander' attached to it to maximize coordination between army and air force. The level of expansion made it necessary to create brigades, composed of at least two wings, and eight were formed between 1916 and 1918. Each wing was made up of two or more squadrons, each squadron of three flights of four aircraft each. Brigades were retitled 'groups' after the war, but the basic organizational structure of the later RAF was already in place well before its formation. The headquarters of the RFC was established in northern France at St Omer, near the Channel coast. The site was a small chateau, overcrowded and improvised. There were no electric lights, and inadequate accommodation for serious staff work. 'My main recollection,' wrote Maurice Baring, recently appointed to the RFC staff, 'is a stuffy office, full of clerks and candles and a deafening noise of typewriters . . . a perpetual stream of guests and a crowd of people sleeping on the floor.'[20] Among the uncomfortable guests was Lt.-Colonel Hugh Trenchard, commander of the RFC (Military Wing) at home, but in November 1914 made commander of the newly formed First Wing. Baring met him at the quayside at Boulogne to take him to St Omer, 'a tall man, with a small head and a Scots Fusiliers cap on'.[21]

Trenchard played a central role in the history of both the RFC and the RAF, but in autumn 1914 he might just as easily have ended any prospect of a major new air service when, as Commander of the Military Wing, he had recommended, with support from Sefton Brancker, Henderson's deputy in London, that the RFC be divided up between the army corps and divisions, each with their own assigned air units, and with no central commander or headquarters.[22] The proposal was quashed after protests from Henderson and his chief-of-staff, Lt.-Colonel Frederick Sykes, who had been Trenchard's predecessor as commander of the Military Wing. There was little love lost between the two men. Sykes was a punctilious military intellectual, at home in the world of politics and diplomacy, more than capable of articulating his views on air strategy and organization, and confident that his view was the right one. He was regarded by some as aloof, cold and devious, by others as too able for his own good.[23] Trenchard, Sykes claimed in his memoirs, was an officer with 'a forceful personality and great drive', but he thought on the bigger issues Trenchard was 'fundamentally wrong' not only in 1914, but later in the war when the two men, one after the other, became chief-of-staff to the fledgling RAF.[24] Trenchard in turn thought Sykes 'secretive . . . kept everything hidden, and never spoke to anyone', though he did concede that Sykes 'was a hard worker and had some brains'.[25] Sykes' dislike of Trenchard persisted long into retirement. He was the only one of Trenchard's surviving contemporaries who refused in the 1950s to be interviewed by Trenchard's biographer.

Other airmen had more generous opinions of a man affectionately known as 'Boom' because of his deep resonant voice. After army service in the Royal Scots Fusiliers in India, South Africa and Nigeria, Trenchard learned to fly at the age of 39 and became Deputy Commander of the Central Flying School, run by the naval aviator Godfrey Paine. When his future chief-of-staff John Salmond arrived at the school as a young trainee pilot he later recalled seeing 'a dark, glowering man with a parchment coloured face and a light behind the eyes'. It was not long, Salmond continued, 'before I knew what the fire meant'.[26] Trenchard was respected as a commander who worked fearlessly without flagging, cared for his crews despite the sacrifices he demanded of them, and single-mindedly defended the organization he commanded. He attracted great loyalty, but colleagues learned that at times he could display a harsh temper and a deliberate brusqueness of manner, masking a lonely inner self. Unlike Sykes, he was ill-at-ease in the world of politics, and instinctively distrusted civilian interference in military affairs. He has always enjoyed the reputation of being inarticulate, in speech and on paper, though he generally knew what he wanted. 'I know I am an untidy talker,' he told his biographer, 'and you may say I have an untidy brain, but in my mind I am persistent and consistent.'[27] His commitment throughout the war was to pursue strategies that would facilitate army victory. As it turned out, he was an unlikely 'father of the RAF'. Up to the last he opposed the formation of the new service in 1918, even after he had reluctantly been pressured into accepting the role of chief-of-staff. Trenchard for his part regarded David Henderson, first Director of Military Aeronautics, as the true father.[28]

In August 1915, Trenchard replaced Henderson as Commander-in-Chief of the RFC in France. His rival Sykes had been posted to the Mediterranean theatre two months before, at the request of the Admiralty, in order to resolve the problems facing the RNAS in the Gallipoli campaign. Henderson had poor health and had relied heavily on Sykes as his chief-of-staff, though, for reasons still not entirely clear, Henderson, like Trenchard, came to distrust his ambitious lieutenant and was happy to see him go.[29] In December 1915 General Douglas Haig, Trenchard's commander when he had been in charge of the First Wing, was appointed Commander-in-Chief of the BEF, and for the next two years a close relationship was forged between the two men as each pursued his own version of the offensive as the only key to victory. Trenchard, like Haig, was prepared to accept high losses as long as the momentum of the offensive could be maintained. 'Air superiority' became the intermediate objective of offensive airpower, because the achievement of superiority would allow aircraft to perform their other critical duties of reconnaissance, artillery spotting and close support without the threat of enemy interception. When Trenchard arrived to command the RFC, however, air superiority was still a distant hope against a German enemy now equipped with the Fokker E.I fighter (or scout, as they were called), which was armed with a forward-firing machine-gun, synchronized with the rotation of the propeller. Losses of aircrew and machines outpaced their replacement. News of the crisis facing the RFC reached the press at home, and for the first time in the war Britain's air services began to catch the attention of politicians and public.

The 'Fokker scourge' as it came to be known in the press was just one of the factors that brought aviation more fully into the limelight. On the night of 19/20 January 1915 the first bombs fell on British soil, when Zeppelin airships attacked the east coast towns of Great Yarmouth, Sheringham and King's Lynn, killing four people and injuring sixteen. The authorities had expected airship raids for some time, but had done little to prepare for them. Over the course of 1915 there were twenty raids in which thirty-seven tons of bombs were dropped, killing 181 people and wounding 455. The first raid that managed to reach London took place on the night of 31 May, when a single airship, LZ38, dropped eighty-nine incendiaries and thirty aerial grenades on the East End, killing nine people.[30] The attacks were indiscriminate, since airships flew at a great height, in the dark, and subject to the vagaries of wind and weather, their crews in a regular state of anxiety about the safety of their isolated airborne station, while fighting against the cold and the occasional lack of sufficient oxygen.[31] As a result of largely random bombing, almost all the casualties were civilians, many of them children, many killed where they lay in bed. Small though the human cost was compared with the campaigns of the next war, the sheer novelty of attacks on British soil against British civilians explains the exaggerated reaction of press and public. After the first modest raid *The Times* condemned an enemy that practised 'ruthless and inhuman destruction', and throughout 1915 there was growing anger at German bombing and deep disquiet about the apparent failure of the armed forces to do anything at all to combat or deter the attacks.[32] There was no way of knowing when a raid was coming. The government and the police were against early warning of impending raids from fear that this would simply create widespread and perhaps unnecessary panic, particularly among war workers; it was also assumed that an audible warning would act as a lure for the airships. Worse still, Zeppelin raids proved a spectacle that encouraged crowds of onlookers, exposing them to the very threat they clustered to watch.

Air defence was not yet a recognized branch of air warfare. The defence of the coasts and inland towns was entrusted to the RNAS in an agreed demarcation between the naval and military wings in 1914, but the Admiralty had given little thought to what air defence entailed. In May 1915 just one anti-aircraft gun, a converted artillery piece, defended London, and there were very few aircraft. The entire RNAS home defence organization even by 1916 employed only 17,341 servicemen and 110 aircraft.[33] Night air defence was rudimentary and dangerous for the crews and, because of the height and speed of the airships, entirely ineffective. Only after the introduction of aircraft with a higher operational ceiling and the development of deadlier explosive and incendiary ammunition did it prove possible on occasion to find and destroy an airship, but most went undetected or unmolested. Against twenty-nine raids counted from 1914 to 1916 there were 166 sorties by British defending aircraft, but 145 never saw the enemy; twenty-one out of the twenty-nine raids were conducted without being sighted at all.[34] The wave of protest against the failure of air defence led to the transfer of home defence to the army in February 1916, with the RFC responsible for all home-based aircraft except those guarding fleet installations. Gradually, over the course of 1916, a more extensive and better-armed air defence system was constructed. In May 1916 the first home defence squadron was activated, and by the end of the year there were eleven squadrons and one night-training squadron. They were eventually formed into 6th Brigade Home Defence, with six wings, eighteen squadrons and ten night-training units.[35] Under army control, a system of lighting restrictions and air raid warnings was introduced. A network of 'Warning Controls' was set up, one for Scotland, six for England and Wales, each run by a Warning Controller who was also the local anti-aircraft defence commander. Cordons of observer posts were set up around London and other industrial centres, linked to the RFC and anti-aircraft commanders by priority telephone, a system not unlike the one later used in the Battle of Britain. Warnings were issued to key personnel, however, not to the public. Some local communities did deliver audible warnings, against police advice, but there remained great confusion over what sounds were permissible if an enemy airship were overhead. Church bells and clock chimes were prohibited, and there were even proposals 'to prohibit singing, whistling or shouting in the streets, even the barking of dogs'. Not until July 1917 did the government finally relent and permit the use of sirens, rattles, whistles and bells.[36]

A dedicated air defence suggested the need for an air force operating independently of the army in the field. The same was true of the long-range bombing of targets beyond the enemy front line, which also implied the possibility at some point of a strategy separate from the army's campaigns on the Western Front and in the Middle East against Turkey. Throughout 1915 and 1916 the RFC and RNAS had conducted small raids against more distant objectives, but the scale was tiny. The Zeppelin raids encouraged the public to call for reprisals and the development of a dedicated bombing force, but the army and navy resisted the idea of attacks carried out simply for revenge. From 1915 onwards senior officers in both services began to explore the possibility, when the technology was available, of conducting long-range raids against industrial and military targets in Germany, with the object of limiting the supply of munitions and reducing the scale of German air attacks. This was the origin of an idea that dominated postwar thinking in the RAF: that the best defence against air attack was an air offensive against the enemy.[37] Even Trenchard, in command of the RFC in France, came during the course of 1916 to accept the idea that aircraft might be used to attack the sources of German supply on the home front and so reduce the pressure on Allied armies. Neither home defence nor long-range bombing necessarily required an air service distinct from the army and navy, but they both involved air power functions that were difficult to reconcile with the insatiable demands of the navy and army for all the aircraft they could get for the direct support of their operations. This emerging sense that airmen would soon be pursuing strategies that did not fit easily with the war on land and at sea prepared the ground for the arguments in 1917 and 1918 over the formation of the RAF, but it did no more than that.

No factor mattered more in preparing the way for a separate air ministry and air force than the damaging competition that developed in the first war years between army and navy demands for aeronautical equipment. Both needed large numbers of aircraft and engines because of the sustained wastage rate, but they competed independently for engineering and industrial resources from a limited number of manufacturers, who indulged in the production of a bewildering array of prototypes. The RFC alone developed or used over 140 different aircraft models and variants.[38] There was no effective coordination of the naval and military air programmes, little standardization, and a persistent war of words between the two sides over allegations of privileged access to contractors. The two services did indeed require different armament, yet competition between them compromised the capacity to produce enough specialized equipment for either force. The alarm over losses in combat spilled over into public concern at the state of the air industry, and in February 1916 Asquith's government established a Joint Air War Committee under the War Minister, Lord Derby, to try to resolve the struggle for resources between the two services. It possessed almost no power to act, and after eight abortive sittings, during which the contest for procurement was aired but not altered, Derby resigned and the committee was wound up.[39] In May, the government decided to appoint an Air Board under the Conservative Leader of the House of Lords, Lord Curzon, but the board was again given no real power to intervene in the disputes between the two services. It did have the effect of demonstrating publicly how far apart the army and navy were on the issue of reconciling their air power aspirations and how dim was the prospect of satisfying public concern about Britain's air policy.

On 23 October Curzon presented the Cabinet with the Board's first and, as it turned out, only report. He used the occasion to lambast the Admiralty in less than diplomatic language for obstructing all efforts to produce a more rational allocation of resources or to take the Board seriously. The RNAS was, in Curzon's view, 'the least efficient branch of the Royal Navy', while the Sea Lords regarded the Board 'as an intruder if not an antagonist'. The First Lord of the Admiralty, Arthur Balfour, rejected Curzon's censure. 'I do not suppose,' he responded, 'that in the whole history of the country any Government department has ever indulged so recklessly in the luxury of inter-departmental criticism.' Curzon had the last word, warning the Cabinet that the Admiralty not only failed to provide assistance to the Board as he had been promised but had displayed throughout a 'resolute antagonism'.[40] The exchange launched almost a decade of remarkably candid, occasionally vituperative, exchanges between the navy and the rest of the air force establishment over the future organization of British military aviation. The conflict was suspended while David Lloyd George succeeded Asquith as Prime Minister in December, but Curzon's objections did not go unheeded. In early 1917 Lloyd George began a radical overhaul of the British air effort that culminated more than a year later in the formation of the RAF. The decision was taken to allocate responsibility for the production of all air equipment to the Minister of Munitions, who was to enforce a rationalization of planning and production. For the first time, there appeared the prospect that an air ministry might be needed to oversee air policy. Lord Curzon had already suggested together with his Board that a single imperial air service and an air ministry would be needed after the war, but it was feared that their creation in the midst of a major conflict would cause too much dislocation.[41] However, in December 1916 the New Ministries and Secretaries Bill decreed that the chair of the Air Board should enjoy equivalent status to a minister, and when a second Board was formally constituted on 6 February 1917 its chair, the industrialist Lord Cowdray, expected that his Board would have proper executive power to influence the evolution of British air policy.[42] In this the new Board was to be disappointed.

The creation of the two Air Boards revealed the extent to which the future organization of British air power was to be governed by political interests as much as by military necessity. For the government, the air mattered first because fear of being bombed might affect public opinion on the war effort, second because the chaos in aircraft production was an issue for the home front economy and the civilians who organized it. For the army and navy, on the other hand, aircraft were overwhelmingly regarded as an auxiliary extension of naval and military power. By the end of 1916 both the RFC and the RNAS were still small branches of their respective services, bearing little comparison with the size or significance of other specialized services such as the Royal Artillery, or the cavalry, or the fleet's gunnery branch. The RFC had 5,982 officers and

51,945 other ranks; the RNAS comprised 2,764 officers and 26,129 supporting personnel.[43] In 1917 both forces were to grow to be much larger, but, although some senior airmen on both sides of the service divide had begun to think that a separate unified force might be desirable, the RAF was not yet visible on the horizon.

## 2

# Battles in the Sky, Battles in Whitehall

For the essential truth on which the Flying Service must be founded is that only aviators understand aviation. The great gain of a separately organized Air Service would be its emancipation from the control of the Admiralty and the War Office, who are very apt to think they know more than they do.

*Hugh Cecil MP, August 1917*[1]

On 1 March 1917, German Gotha G.V bombers, flying from air bases in German-occupied Belgium, dropped nine high-explosive bombs on the Kent coastal town of Broadstairs, three of them falling in the sea. On 5 April the Kent coast was hit again: four bombs fell on Broadstairs this time, one on Ramsgate and three near Sandwich. No one was killed. These probing raids against easy-to-reach coastal targets signalled the onset of a German bombing campaign by aeroplane rather than by airship. Insignificant as the first raids proved to be, the War Office worried about the implications of operations that 'exhibit entirely new possibilities in aerial warfare'.[2] More than any other factor, it was the German decision to begin this small-scale bomber offensive that triggered the British government's move to form an independent air service.

The decision by the German High Command to switch

from airship to aeroplane bombing coincided with the authorization in February 1917 of unrestricted submarine warfare against Allied shipping. Both were gambles in a year when the German war effort was stretched taut, and military leaders searched for less-orthodox strategies in order to put pressure on the British government and public to withdraw from the war. The gamble rested on the hope that even with a modest number of aircraft – there were just twenty-three Gotha bombers at the start of 1917 – a crisis of morale might be triggered among the war-weary British population. The same calculation had persuaded German leaders to allow Lenin and his revolutionary entourage to travel in a sealed train across Germany to Russia following the overthrow of the Tsarist regime in February 1917, in the hope that revolutionary crisis would undermine the Russian war effort too. But by the time the first major bombing raid was launched in daylight on 25 May, with all twenty-three Gothas attacking targets on the Kent coast, the United States had declared war on Germany, making it even less probable that bombing seaside towns would quickly eliminate British belligerency. The raid on 25 May caused severe damage and killed ninety-two people. Although RFC and RNAS aeroplanes were sent up to intercept, the Gothas flew too high and none was hit. The next raid, by twenty-two aircraft, struck the Thames Estuary on 5 June. Finally, on 13 June fourteen bombers reached London in mid-morning, where they dropped their load in a broad swathe across the central and eastern areas of the city, out of range of anti-aircraft guns and enemy aircraft. One bomb hit a school in Poplar and exploded in an infant class, killing all the small children inside. It was the deadliest raid of the war, unexpected and without warning. A total of 145 people were killed, 382 injured, most of them in a handful of East End boroughs, but nothing matched the horror expressed across the capital at the slaughter of the eighteen infants in Poplar. Their funeral a week later sparked a deep emotional response and fuelled an outburst of popular anti-German sentiment and calls for reprisals in kind.[3] Anger was directed equally at the military authorities for the complete failure of the air defence system and at the government for maintaining their refusal to issue warnings of oncoming raids. The Home Secretary announced in the House of Commons on 28 June that it was still considered impracticable to issue adequate warnings, but the result was to increase public fear that the raids would only get worse.

The raids in fact developed very slowly as aircraft were repaired or new ones introduced, and the right meteorological conditions were essential. Not until 7 July 1917 was London attacked again, but this raid has generally been taken as the point at which the government, alarmed by the growing public protest, began a search for a solution that ended with the creation of an air ministry and the RAF. There is no doubt that the second major raid on London did finally prompt the government to react to the public's uneasy anger at the supine response to this and earlier raids. The Home Secretary at last agreed that warnings could be issued, signalled by 'sound rockets' or 'sound bombs' fired from police and fire stations or by policemen with whistles and rattles. On 16 July the Local Government Board announced that welfare aid and compensation would be paid to surviving victims of the raids.[4] Although the raid inflicted fewer casualties than the one in June (fifty-three dead and 182 injured), once again the failure of the guns or defending aircraft to inhibit the raiders exacerbated the sense of outrage in the capital. Rioting and looting were directed at any premises that looked alien. The press called for tough reprisals against the German civil population. On 10 July Parliament met in special session to discuss the raids, and the following day Lloyd George established a small committee to investigate the whole air situation, consisting of himself and the South African Lt.-General Jan Smuts, who had come to Britain as an invited member of the Imperial War Cabinet.[5] The Prime Minister's Committee on Air Organisation and Home Defence Against Air Raids was further reduced to a one-man show once it became clear that Lloyd George intended to play only a passive role. It was Lloyd George's intention to ask the MP Hugh Cecil to join the committee, but Smuts persuaded him that all that was needed was a secretary, and he proposed the Conservative MP Leo Amery. For expert advice Smuts relied chiefly on the Director General of Military Aeronautics, David Henderson.[6]

Smuts has often been regarded as an odd choice for an assignment that raised significant political and military issues for Britain's continued war effort. He arrived in Britain from South Africa in April after two years in command of British Empire forces in East Africa. Although he was a former enemy in the South African War of 1899–1902, he was a distinguished political and military figure who had played an important part in healing the rift between Dutch and British colonists when South Africa became a unitary state in 1910. He had a reputation as something of a military intellectual. He arrived in Britain at a point of mounting pessimism among Britain's political and military leadership about the outcome of the war and the social costs it imposed on the population.[7] For Lloyd George, Smuts seems to have been a respected outsider, whose advice would be fresher and less prejudiced than that of his military leaders and political colleagues, but he turned down the prime minister's offer to take up command in the Middle

East on the ground that he did not want to run an essentially defensive campaign, and as a result he was present in London when the first bombs fell.[8]

He was interested in air power because, like other air enthusiasts, he believed that the air effort properly directed might have 'decisive importance' for the outcome of the war. On 5 June he met Winston Churchill, who had been out of office since the Dardanelles disaster. He tried, almost certainly at Lloyd George's instigation, to persuade Churchill that, if he were to be offered the choice of running the Ministry of Munitions or a proposed Air Ministry, he should accept the latter, where his 'constructive ability and initiative' would prove more useful. Smuts reported to Lloyd George that Churchill would take the offer only if he were given real scope to develop a new 'Air Service' and control over appointments.[9] Lloyd George, after much hesitation given the opposition of many of his coalition partners, finally did offer Churchill the choice of Munitions or Air, without informing Lord Cowdray, who already held ministerial rank as President of the Air Board. 'I said at once,' Churchill later wrote, 'that I preferred Munitions.'[10] The appointment was announced on 18 July, and for the moment the creation of an air ministry was postponed. It is evident that Smuts was already involved in political discussions about changes to the organization of British air power even before the raids in June and July, which makes his appointment to run the new air committee less anomalous. Two days after his meeting with Churchill, Smuts watched the first major Gotha raid from the roof of the Savoy Hotel in the Strand, where he was staying. He later toured the bombed areas.[11]

Smuts produced for the War Cabinet two reports, not one, as is often suggested. The first was circulated on 19 July 1917 and concerned the question of more effective defence for London. The Army Commander-in-Chief of Home Forces, Field Marshal John French, had already written to Henderson following the 7 July raid to express the army's disappointment at the failure of guns and aircraft to obstruct the attack; the Army Council recommended a single centralized air defence system, bringing together observation, communication, antiaircraft artillery and aeroplanes under one commander.[12] This view was almost certainly passed on by Henderson to Smuts, whose first report also recommended to the War Cabinet a unitary defensive system for London. A month later the London Air Defence Area was established under the command of Brigadier-General Edward Ashmore, a career artilleryman who learned to fly in 1912 and was briefly commander of an RFC wing under Trenchard.[13] The Second Report was presented on 17 August 1917, and it is this document that is usually referred to as the 'Smuts Report'. The conclusions clearly owed something to views that Smuts already had about the future possibilities of air power, but the recommendations that British air policy and air operations would best be handled by an air ministry, an air staff and a unified air service were arrived at only after Smuts had listened to and accepted the arguments of others.[14] Henderson was a key contributor. On 19 July he drafted a lengthy memorandum on the 'Organisation of the Air Service' for the committee, which laid out the long history of friction between the RFC and the RNAS and the limitations imposed on the second Air Board by the determination of the army and navy to keep air policy in their separate hands. Henderson concluded that the only way to overcome an illogical situation was the formation of 'a complete department and a complete united service dealing with all operations in the air', a recommendation that formed the hub of the later report. Henderson ended with a warning that proved only too prescient: there would be 'the most violent controversies over the petty details'.[15]

Of the two major recommendations, the creation of an air ministry with a consultative board, equivalent to the Admiralty and the War Office, was the least contentious. The idea of a separate air ministry had circulated among politicians since it was first raised in the House of Lords by the air enthusiast Lord Montagu of Beaulieu in March 1916, where his motion in favour was defeated.[16] Even among those who supported the idea, including the President of the First Air Board, Lord Curzon, and Lord Cowdray, President of the Second Board, the view prevailed that the creation of a new ministry at the height of the war effort might prove too disruptive. But in July 1917, Cowdray wrote at length to Smuts to explain that his Board had simply been unable to establish any control over policy and to recommend that an air ministry with its own war staff should after all be set up at once.[17] Churchill, now in overall charge of aeronautical supply as Minister of Munitions, discussed the whole issue with Smuts and Cowdray in early August and endorsed the idea of a new War Staff for a strengthened Air Board or ministry, a view that he passed on to Lloyd George two weeks before the Second Report.[18] What both meant by a 'war staff' or what responsibilities it might have were unclear, but the army and navy leadership assumed that an air ministry would act simply as a 'trainer and provider' of air crew and equipment rather than direct operations, while the army and navy would retain absolute control over selecting and utilizing the naval and military air forces assigned to them. The War Office accepted the proposal for an air ministry only on the proviso that the army would still decide what air supplies it needed and should be 'free to use them in their own way without any interference from the Air Ministry'.[19]

The more radical proposal in the Second Report was the creation of a single unified 'Air Service' run by an Air Staff. Here Smuts relied almost entirely on Henderson's advice, since neither Cowdray nor Churchill, otherwise staunch supporters of the idea of a new ministry and staff, argued for the creation of an entirely new service, to be created under the extreme conditions of a war that Britain might still lose. The argument for a separate air service rested in the end very little on the importance of providing more effective air defence, even if that was what Lloyd George had expected. Instead, the issue of a unified service rested on the contention, strongly supported by Smuts, that aircraft technology had now reached the point where it was possible to inflict long-range 'independent' damage on the German home front. The report concluded with the well-known speculation that 'continuous and intense pressure against the chief industrial centres of the enemy as well as on his lines of communications may form the determining factor in bringing about peace'. Smuts also endorsed bombing in the Middle East theatre. He hoped that Allied air superiority would enable air forces to cut Turkey's fragile communications network and finally 'wrest victory and peace' from the dangerous stalemate that currently existed. For Smuts and his advisers, as for the German leadership, air power seemed to offer a way out of the strategic dead end both countries had arrived at in 1917.[20]

Supporters for the idea of a long-range bombing campaign could be found in both the navy and the army, although the military and naval leadership assumed that long-range operations would be designed to help surface forces achieve their goals more effectively, rather than usher in a new age of

independent air power. Arguments in favour of bombing mul-
tiplied in the autumn of 1917, not least because it would at the
same time assuage public demands for retaliation against German raids and dampen down social protest. In the discussions
before the Second Report was published, it was widely
assumed that there would be an aircraft surplus the following
year, thanks to the effort of Sir William Weir, the Scottish engineering industrialist who had been recruited in January 1917
to run the aeronautics branch of the Ministry of Munitions.[21]
The 'Surplus Air Fleet', as it came to be called, was something
of a phantom, since the army and navy would happily have
taken all the aircraft available, rather than see a fraction of
them siphoned off for independent operations. Weir did succeed during the course of 1917 in more than doubling the
output of finished aircraft – 14,168 against 6,099 in 1916.[22] This
was done by cutting back the very large number of different aircraft models in production, from fifty-five in spring 1917 to
thirty a year later. Aircraft firms were compelled to shift from
the haphazard and small-scale pattern of production to more
efficient manufacturing units, each one monitored by a Production Officer to ensure prompt delivery and good practice. For
1918 Weir promised to deliver more than 11,000 aircraft between
March and June, from which the 'Surplus Air Fleet' could be
supplied alongside the demands of the army and navy.[23]

The plans for bombing Germany transformed the way
modern warfare was conceived. They made explicit the idea
that the civilian home front was ineluctably linked with the
overall national war effort and could legitimately be regarded
as an object for attack. Military and industrial targets supplying the means to wage war were a priority, but from the outset
the campaign against domestic civilian targets was also expected to have a demoralizing effect on the enemy workforce,

although the result in London had been to make the population vengeful and angry rather than despondent. The effect, it
was hoped, would be to reduce war output through interrup-
tions caused by alarms and raids and a consequent increase in
absenteeism, as German bombing had achieved, if only briefly,
during 1916 and 1917.[24] Like Smuts, those who pressed for independent operations saw bombing as perhaps decisive for the
outcome of the war. Rear-Admiral Mark Kerr, one of the
navy's foremost advocates of bombing, warned the Air Board
that 'the country who first strikes with its big bombing squadrons of hundreds of machines at the enemy's vital spots, will
win the war.'[25] Victory, wrote Kerr in a separate note, was now
about interrupting or destroying the supplies and communications of the enemy, not about defeat in the field. In these early
arguments about the independent use of aircraft lay the roots
of what soon came to be called 'total war', a struggle between
entire societies, soldiers and civilians alike. Air power exercised independently meant waging war, as the Liberal MP Sir
Henry Norman put it, 'upon new strategic principles'.[26]

The Second Report produced by Smuts was acted upon almost at once. On 24 August, in Lloyd George's absence, a
meeting of the War Cabinet was called to reach a decision on
whether or not to accept it. The minutes show strong support
for the creation of an air ministry, but more guarded judge-
ments about the creation of a unified air service. Churchill
was strongly supportive, not least because he hoped that
American entry into the war would mean additional aircraft
for the 'Surplus Air Fleet' and United States participation in
the air war. Strongly opposed was the First Lord of the Admiralty, Eric Geddes, who on the advice of the Admiralty Board
rejected both a ministry and a united air force on the grounds
that the air war at sea was fundamentally different from the

air support given to the British armies. The Chief of the Imperial General Staff, Sir William Robertson, wanted the War Office to retain the right to determine its own aerial requirements, but his proposed amendment along those lines was rejected. Both army and navy were overruled. The Cabinet voted to accept the report; a new committee was to be set up, again under Smuts, to arrange the coordination and amalgamation of the RNAS and the RFC, together with the necessary legislation.[27]

There is little record of Lloyd George's own motives in initiating the two reports, though they were almost certainly expedient. It seems likely that he thought the change might be no more than a wartime improvisation that would not need to survive the end of the war. His priorities were short-term and political: first, he wanted to be seen by the public to be responding to popular anxiety about the air war, and to be exploring new strategic avenues away from the stalemate in the trenches, currently exposed in the brutal and ineffective offensive at Passchendaele; second, the decision to take back political control of the air services under an air ministry run by civilians was a further episode in the contest between military and civilian direction of the war effort, which Lloyd George wanted to see resolved in favour of the politicians. For both of these reasons, the creation of the Air Ministry and the RAF must be understood as a direct product of political calculation, not of military insistence.

Smuts now found himself as the busy chair of four further committees: an Air Raids Committee for issues of civil defence, an Air Reorganisation Committee for drawing up the necessary legislation and organizational structures for the combined air service, the Air Policy Committee for addressing the question of what aircraft were needed and for which roles, and finally on 8 October 1917 a War Priorities Committee to decide where resources should best be allocated for strategic impact, which Smuts, with Weir's support, used as a platform to argue the case for shifting resources to the new air arm.[28] Nevertheless, the Cabinet decision did not create overnight either a ministry or a new air force. The flurry of activity masked a growing confusion about how a new ministry should be set up and with what responsibilities, and over the extent to which the new unitary air service would or would not still be subject to the navy and army that they served. Throughout the year, both the navy and the army air services had grown in size and competence in their roles as auxiliary to surface forces. The RFC won back air superiority over the British section of the front in France during the course of 1917; the RNAS had improved aircraft and tactics for the anti-submarine campaign, which was a strategic priority for 1917. Neither service wanted a situation where these improvements in air support might be compromised.

Of the two branches, the navy was most hostile to the decision for amalgamation, though not uniformly so. Admiral David Beatty, Commander-in-Chief of the Grand Fleet, told Geddes before the Cabinet meeting that the Royal Navy was 'too parochial' in its views and that he broadly favoured the new ministry and the new air force. But Beatty also assumed that where air and fleet operated together, the air service must always be 'an adjunct and servant' of the navy, controlled and commanded by the naval staff.[29] The First Sea Lord, Admiral John Jellicoe, was adamantly opposed to what he viewed as a 'mistaken organisation', in which nothing would be gained and a great deal lost once an air staff had begun to redirect aircraft supplies away from the army and navy to meet their own independent needs.[30] The detailed and lengthy memoranda generated by the Admiralty response to the Smuts report highlighted the navy's concern that the specialized and specific functions in air-sea warfare could only be managed by naval personnel who understood the training and operational requirements of a naval air force. This was not an unreasonable position, given that the RNAS did require a different kind of training for long oversea flights, difficult landings on the first improvised seaplane and aircraft carriers, and a high level of navigational skill. A few days before the Second Report was submitted, the captain of HMS *Campania*, one of the first converted aircraft carriers, complained to the Admiralty that the pilots supplied by the joint training scheme were hopelessly unprepared for naval work. Most had never flown with a passenger and found it difficult to accommodate the observer's needs; most had little familiarity with the use of a compass; few actually knew how to start their engine, or how to throttle down and stop it.[31] The need for specialized and prolonged training remained a central argument for the Royal Navy throughout its long postwar efforts to kill off RAF control of their aircraft.

The attitude of the army to the new flying service was governed by rather different concerns. By 1917, offensive counter-force operations and ground support for troops had assumed much greater significance. Operational summaries for the RFC in 1917 show aircraft engaged in reconnaissance, aerial photography, artillery spotting and extensive bombing of enemy air bases and rail communications.[32] The RFC was constantly in combat, where for the RNAS combat at sea was a rarity. RNAS squadrons stationed on the French Channel coast flew regularly in support of army operations, where they acted like RFC squadrons. In May 1917 the RNAS aircraft assembled in No. 3 Wing for bombing targets in Germany were disbanded and sent to assist the land battle.[33] The BEF leadership wanted to maintain the momentum of operational success in the air and, like the navy, wanted to control air units attached to the army and to be able to determine how many aircraft were needed. But in contrast to the RNAS, the RFC was larger and better endowed by 1917 with aircraft and air crew and an extensive logistics system. Amalgamation might well mean, as the navy feared, that naval aviation would become a junior partner. Army attitudes were as a result ambivalent in all except one significant case. Douglas Haig, the Commander-in-Chief of the BEF, was an enthusiastic champion of the RFC and firmly in favour of developing a greater long-range bombing capability, and he did not actively oppose the conclusions in the Second Report. Even with a separate air force, Haig assumed that he would still be able to dictate what the army wanted the air force to do, an argument that the Chief of the Imperial General Staff had tried to get the Cabinet to accept in August.[34] The idea that air power might end the war on its own, however, Haig dismissed as 'mere assertion unsupported by facts'.[35]

The sternest opponent of the proposal for a separate air force was Hugh Trenchard. In this there is a profound irony, because two years later Trenchard was instrumental in ensuring that the RAF retain its independence from the army and navy, and subsequently became the champion of the air force against all efforts to break it up. In 1917, however, Trenchard saw the situation differently. By the autumn he had succeeded in turning the RFC into a force capable of retaining air superiority, armed with a clutch of improved aircraft and poised, if the promised supply of 'surplus' equipment materialized, to conduct long-range bombing operations in order to weaken German resistance at the front. His priority was to assist the army in achieving a victory on land under his command, and to resist reforms that threatened to undermine that aim. In late August he sent a detailed memorandum to Robertson setting out 'reasons against creating a separate Air Service'. His principal concern was the effect on military efficiency brought about by the creation of a third competitive service after years of strife with the RNAS. Worse still was the introduction of political control of aviation:

> An Air Ministry with a civilian head and uncontrolled by any outside Naval and Military opinion, exposed as it would inevitably be to popular and fractional clamour, would be very liable to lose its sense of proportion and be drawn towards the spectacular, such as bombing reprisals and home defence, at the expense of providing the essential means of co-operation with our Naval and Military Forces.[36]

In another report a few weeks later, Trenchard returned to the theme that union would not only undermine the principle that the navy and army should necessarily control their own auxiliary air force, but would inevitably lead to 'friction and serious danger of loss of efficiency'.[37] Nor could Trenchard understand why no senior RFC officer had been invited to attend Smuts' committee on the Air Service. He deplored the probability that the new service would be imposed on him willy-nilly: 'I do not quite understand why these changes are continually going on in the Air Service when there is nothing wrong with the Service except the quantity of material supplied.'[38] When his chief-of-staff, John Salmond, was appointed to replace Henderson in October as Director General of Military Aeronautics, Trenchard reminded him that his priority was to serve the needs of the military: 'Remember that we are part of the Army and are not trying to run a separate show at their expense.'[39]

It is unlikely that Trenchard could have prevented the creation of the new air service, much though he might have wished it, because he neither wanted nor sought political support in London for his views, nor an alliance with naval critics. The committees set up under Smuts worked away to resolve the many practical and administrative issues involved in amalgamation. In September Smuts established an Air Council which would replace the Air Board once the Air Ministry and an air service had been approved by Parliament, but progress was slow.[40] The factor that ended any uncertainty in the minds of the politicians about the wisdom of the decision taken in August was supplied once again by the German enemy, when the Gotha bombers, accompanied now by the new four-engine Zeppelin-Staaken R. VI aircraft, whose huge size earned it the nickname 'Giant', returned in late September to recommence the campaign. The raids began on 24 September and continued with one interruption until 1 October, but the bombers came this time at night rather than during the day. What came to be called the 'Harvest Moon Raids' had a much greater impact than the two major raids in June and July because they continued night after night, with the bombs scattered quite indiscriminately, just as they had been in the earlier Zeppelin raids. The raids were nevertheless modest in scale. Few of the attacking aircraft, as in June and July, actually reached London. During the first raid, on 24 September, only three aircraft bombed the capital: one dropped three 50 kilo bombs and six incendiaries, two more between them dropped ten 50 kilo bombs and eleven incendiaries, one of which destroyed a gallery in the Royal Academy's Burlington House. The remaining raids were small-scale and random. Most incendiaries were observed to fall harmlessly on roadways, backyards and open spaces. Casualties as a result were remarkably low, given the unpredictable nature of the raiding, with forty-seven deaths and injury to a further 226 (though six deaths and sixty-seven injuries were caused by the debris from anti-aircraft shells).[41] The impact on public morale was nevertheless as disconcerting as it had been in the summer.[42]

Rumours had circulated for some time that the German air forces were planning an obliterating attack on the capital, a fantasy from which the military were not immune. In October 1917 Rear-Admiral Kerr, relying on intelligence supplied by Britain's Italian ally, warned the Air Board that the Germans were planning a knockout blow with 4,000 bomber aircraft (more like forty, Trenchard scoffed, who was much closer to the truth).[43] The popular view was pessimistic. After the first raid, thousands of Londoners searched every night for shelter in tunnels or basements, or camped out in Richmond Park and other open spaces. They also began to congregate in stations on the London Underground – an estimated 120,000 on the second night of raiding. On two nights when there proved to be no raids, queues had already formed by 5.30 in the evening. The Home Office assumed that many were 'the poorer type of aliens' from London's East End. 'They not only went there in entire families,' claimed a later report, 'diminutive girls or boys carrying the latest baby, but they took with them supplies of provisions, pillows and bedding . . . together with their cat or their dog, their parrot or their pet canary'.[44] By the end of the raids, an estimated 300,000 clustered into the stations each night. The effect on production was temporary but severe. At one of the country's major clothing companies in the East End, workers failed to turn up during the day, and output sank from 40,000 suits to 5,000. The managing director uncharitably attributed the crisis to the fact that 90 per cent of his employees were women, 'easily frightened and liable to panic', and the other ten per cent Jewish aliens 'who were even more liable to panic than the women', though the fears were more than justified because the factories were almost entirely constructed of glass to allow more light and had no available shelters. Even at the Woolwich arsenal, better prepared for disruption, more than 70 per cent of the workforce was absent during the raids, cutting output to a fraction.[45]

This time the War Cabinet was more alarmed by the public response. On 1 October Trenchard was summoned back from France to attend a meeting to discuss the retaliatory bombing of Germany. He was asked to set up a unit of bombers at Ochey, near Nancy in eastern France, to bomb German industrial targets in the Saar region. On 2 October Henderson wrote to Haig informing him that, in response to the bombing of London, the War Cabinet insisted on inaugurating the long-range bombing of Germany at the earliest moment possible. With some reluctance, since neither the bases nor the aircraft were yet in place, Trenchard and Haig complied, though Trenchard even on this issue could not refrain from voicing his objections: 'the weather may break, the moon is going, and we are being rushed into doing it with short range machines which will not have the desired effect on PRUSSIAN towns.'[46] On 16–17 October a force of twenty-two aircraft in two raids dropped sixteen bombs on factories in and around Saarbrücken. The crews claimed that at least eight bombs had fallen on the Burbach ironworks, causing fire damage, but effective intelligence on the results was almost non-existent.[47] The tiny force was organized as the 41st Wing (later 8th Brigade) and placed under the command of Lt.-Colonel Cyril Newall, the future RAF chief-of-staff at the start of the Second

World War. As Trenchard had predicted, its achievements were negligible. The standard light bombers, the De Havilland DH4 and the Farman Experimental F.E.2B, with its open-sided fuselage, could carry little more than 250 pounds of bombs.[48] To fly in difficult winter weather, principally by night, against distant targets, was a considerable challenge; 'no great accuracy,' concluded a GHQ report on the campaign, 'can be expected . . .'[49] The 41st Wing had only three squadrons, one of them from the RNAS, until the formation of the RAF in April 1918. Over the period from October 1917 to June 1918, the force dropped just 129 tons of bombs (fifty-four tons by day, seventy-five by night), and suffered accumulating losses of 13 per cent of the aircraft employed. Intelligence surveys of the damage concluded that material effects on enemy rail traffic 'cannot be said to have been very great', nor the damage to the Saarland steel industry and the bombed chemical works ('material damage has been small').[50] The raids were nevertheless reported in the British press as evidence that the RFC was now retaliating in kind to the German bombs.

The September raids also ended any hesitation about the merits of establishing a new air force and a new ministry. The necessary legislation was drafted and submitted to Parliament, where it was debated on 12 November. 'It is the spirit and object of this Bill,' the Attorney-General, F. E. Smith, told the Commons, 'that the Air Service shall be recognized as an entirely distinguishable Service . . . all the conditions of warfare have been revolutionized by the calling into existence of a new arm.'[51] The Air Force (Constitution) Act was passed into law on 29 November 1917. The preamble stated that 'It shall be lawful for His Majesty [George V] to raise and maintain a force, to be called the Air Force . . .' but the personnel were in the first instance to be recruited for a period of no more than four years, a decision that was to hamper postwar efforts to maintain the RAF as a separate service. The Act empowered the creation of an Air Council presided over by the new Secretary of State for Air, both to be in place by January 1918, when the Second Air Board would relinquish all its functions and personnel to the new ministry.[52]

There remained the politically awkward issue of who would become the first Air Minister. After Churchill's refusal, the natural choice was the current president of the Air Board, Lord Cowdray, who had worked successfully to turn the Board's organization into a semi-ministry. For reasons which remain unclear, Lloyd George decided to sound out Lord Northcliffe, the press baron, as a possible candidate. Northcliffe was an odd choice, given the persistent hostility to the government displayed in his newspapers, and it may be that Lloyd George was less interested in his qualifications for running an air ministry than in securing Northcliffe's collaboration. This proved a profound misjudgement. On 16 November 1917 Northcliffe took the tactless path of publishing a letter in *The Times* publicly declining the prime minister's 'repeated invitation' to take charge of the new department. 'I can do better work,' he continued, 'if I maintain my independence and am not gagged by a loyalty that I do not feel towards the whole of your Administration.'[53] Cowdray learned only by the letter in *The Times* that he was to be replaced; he resigned the same day, making sure his resignation letter was published in the same paper. Lloyd George apologized on behalf of the War Cabinet, but the damage was done and Cowdray left public life (though he later endowed the RAF Club in London's Piccadilly with £100,000). It was not to be the only time that political and personal controversy surrounded the new offices created by the legislation.

Lloyd George then offered the post to Northcliffe's brother, Harold Harmsworth, Lord Rothermere, owner of Associated Newspapers and the successful proprietor of the *Daily Mirror* and the *Sunday Pictorial*. Northcliffe had shown a keen interest in aviation, but Rothermere's qualifications for the job were minimal. He had helped to run the army clothing department in 1916–17, a role in which he was regarded as a success. Lord Beaverbrook, his fellow press baron, later suggested that Rothermere accepted the offer as a token of political appeasement after Northcliffe's brusque rejection, but his motives still remain unclear.[54] His appointment was confirmed following the formal announcement of Cowdray's resignation on 26 November. Lloyd George may once again have hoped that recruiting one of the Harmsworth brothers might stifle press criticism, but Rothermere had little political experience and only a layman's grasp of the way air power had developed over the course of the war. His newspapers were used to agitate for heavy retaliatory raids on Germany, beyond any operational possibility.[55]

The obvious choice for the new post of Chief of the Air Staff was Trenchard, but his opposition to a new air service and his complete lack of experience in the world of politics and administration made him a difficult choice. When the post of Director General of Military Aeronautics had become vacant following Henderson's retirement through ill-health, Trenchard rejected the idea that he should replace him: 'I am no good in an office, and I am afraid that I would not carry through the work at home with all the different departments as well as other men would.'[56] Rothermere and Northcliffe invited Trenchard to a meeting at the Ritz Hotel in central London on 16 December 1917, and after hours of often bitter argument, he accepted the post against all his better instincts. His parting shot as he left the room at 3.00 in the morning was to remind his hosts that 'I am neither a good writer nor a good talker.'[57] He later claimed that he had accepted the post only to forestall a newspaper campaign against Haig's conduct of the war, a man for whom he had unreserved respect. 'I thought by doing this,' he wrote, 'I might be able to help Haig and victory.'[58] But it is clear that he also believed a senior airman was needed to secure the future interests of the air services in the face of political intervention and that no one else had the necessary rank or experience to be able to do so. Trenchard and Haig both hoped that he would be allowed to retain command of the RFC as well as his role as chief-of-staff. Salmond was sent back to France to act as Trenchard's deputy, but on the eve of his new appointment Trenchard still saw himself as commander of the RFC. The War Cabinet rejected the idea, despite Haig's insistence, correctly as it turned out, that the following four months might be the 'most critical of the whole war'.[59] On 18 January Trenchard was confirmed as the new Chief of the Air Staff, with Rear-Admiral Mark Kerr as his deputy. John Salmond became the new commander of the RFC.

The task facing Rothermere and the new Air Council and Air Staff was a formidable one. No other fighting power established an independent air force during the war. The new service rested heavily on established practices and personnel from both the RNAS and the RFC, both of whose commanders would be on the new Air Council. This did not prevent the Admiralty from continuing its efforts to torpedo the new organization by insisting on retaining as much control as it could over the use of naval aircraft and the command and discipline of naval air personnel. The creation of a single service, as Geddes wrote some months later, was only accepted 'against [the Admiralty's] own views and under protest'.[60] In January the new Air Ministry complained to the Admiralty that the navy's request to keep the right to command and discipline all airmen engaged on operations with the fleet would make the ministry 'a controlling body . . . with nothing to control'.[61] Efforts at compromise still left the Admiralty on the eve of the transfer to the new air service in command of all airmen engaged in operations, and subject to naval discipline, while a newly created Admiral Commanding Aircraft would run the air service of the Grand Fleet with advice from an Air Force officer – in effect creating a naval service within the air service. The Air Council failed to modify the Admiralty claims, and in consequence the tension between the navy's view of the new air force and the claims of the Air Ministry remained unresolved even after its official formation.[62]

The Air Council nevertheless worked on the assumption that a unitary air service was a possibility, even if it would take months to work out the necessary details on discipline, pay, ranks, pensions and administration. As David Henderson had observed the year before, the devil was in the details. The first problem was to try to accommodate the new Ministry. Rothermere inherited the Hotel Cecil on the Strand in central London, where the Air Board had been housed. The requisitioned hotel gave the whole enterprise a more temporary character than it needed. Rothermere later complained that the hotel was a model of inefficiency, with a myriad of small bedrooms on endless corridors, with the result that 'supervision is difficult', and much unnecessary communication was needed between offices that were physically too far apart.[63] To add to the problems, Weir, appointed as the Ministry of Munitions representative on the Air Council, requisitioned the upper floors of the nearby Savoy Hotel (leaving the restaurant still functioning) but with hundreds of administrative officials and technical officers spread across the hotel's bedroom accommodation.[64] The most pressing issue facing the Council was to decide when the new air service should come into operation, but the unpredictable nature of the many obstacles to establishing a new service in wartime made it difficult to be precise. As late as early March the Council was still debating when it might happen, though the beginning of April was the preferred date. Trenchard warned that acting too hastily 'might cause dislocation on the Fronts', which he was always anxious to avoid. Perhaps aware of the drawback to April Fools' Day as the choice, Godfrey Paine, one of the RNAS representatives, suggested midnight on 31 March, if the Treasury agreed that this was the official start of the new financial year. Not until 8 March did the Council finally confirm that 1 April would be the date when the new air service would begin.[65]

There was again uncertainty about what the force should be called. Most of those involved talked and wrote about an 'Air Service'. The legislation for the first time defined it as an 'Air Force', a term that had been used rarely. But because the Act had specified 'His Majesty's Air Force' there was no possibility of adding 'Royal' without the king's warrant. The Air Council wondered whether, like the Royal Navy, where the 'Royal' had been accepted by usage rather than royal approval, the Air Force could simply add the extra adjective. Legal advice was sought to see whether or how the King might authorize the use of 'Royal', or to learn if it could be done informally without the King's explicit consent.[66] The title clearly mattered given the atmosphere of insecurity surrounding the new service, but the issue assumed an exaggerated importance. On 19 February the Council was informed that the King had happily consented to the title 'Royal Air Force', the name it has borne ever since.[67] A royal warrant was prepared for the new service, and on 22 March the King approved an Order in Council uniting the two air services and authorizing the transfer of personnel from the navy and army for a period not exceeding four years.[68] After a complex gestation, the Royal Air Force was to be born ten days later, on 1 April 1918.

The intervening days saw the new force plunged into drama. On 19 March Trenchard had unexpectedly tendered his resignation after just two months in his new office. He told Rothermere the day before that he could not tolerate the fact that air force matters, which he regarded as properly the concern of the chief-of-staff, were discussed or decided on without his advice or his presence. He cited several examples to illustrate that, in his view, 'the situation created is an impossible one'. Although Rothermere tried to assure him that he had great confidence in his chief-of-staff, a view at odds with the awkwardly hostile relationship evident between the two men, Trenchard asked to be relieved of his position.[69] Rothermere invited him to wait for formal acceptance of his resignation until after the founding of the RAF on 1 April to avoid public concern, and Trenchard reluctantly agreed. The explicit reasons for his decision to resign lay in his frustration at Rothermere's practices as a minister. In January, he complained to Haig that Rothermere was 'quite ignorant of the needs or working of the Air Service'; Haig noted in his diary Trenchard's judgement that 'the Air Service cannot survive as an independent Ministry.'[70] Weeks before sending his resignation letter, he had considered abandoning a job he had not wanted. On 10 February he wrote to his replacement as the commander of the RFC, John Salmond, complaining that the ministry he now worked for was 'ridiculous' and 'inefficient' in the way its numerous offices were set up.[71] Three days later, he sent Salmond a second private letter, regretting what he had done, and deploring the decision to create a separate air force:

> I come against snags every day in making this Air Service and the more I think of it the more I think what a ghastly mistake has been made in trying to make an Air Service during this war. It is almost an impossibility to run . . . I miss very much the small self-contained Staff in France . . . It is impossible for me to impress myself on them as a Dictator. I hope to do this in six or eight months' time . . . I am still on the brink of stopping, but if I do I do not know whether I shall be doing right to the Flying Corps.[72]

Rothermere's treatment of Trenchard might well have been the straw that broke the camel's back, but Trenchard had been right the year before when he said 'I am no good in an office', and the first few weeks in the Hotel Cecil had confirmed his judgement. He was a natural commander, used to military structures of command. In a ministry, even one devoted to a military service, command was elusive. On the Air Council he was one voice among many, with less influence, so he thought, than the ministerial appointments, and always subject to the veto of the new minister. He was, Rothermere observed after Trenchard announced his resignation, a prime case of 'a square peg in a round hole', though Trenchard could well have returned the compliment.[73]

The commander in Trenchard must have longed to be back in France when, two days after he had sent his resignation letter, the German army launched the last major offensive on the Western Front, the *Kaiserschlacht*, the Kaiser's battle. The British length of the front was pushed back in disarray, and every squadron of the RFC was in action giving ground support to the retreating army, joined by those RNAS squadrons stationed near the coast, uniting the two services in the field through the military crisis. Trenchard was briefly back in his element, communicating with Salmond and the RFC staff without reference to Rothermere or the Air Council.[74] The Council minutes, as a result, give little or no sense of the crisis in France. Nor did the air forces, battling away in French skies, have any hint that Trenchard was about to resign. The creation of the RAF was eclipsed entirely by the desperate efforts to stem the German tide. A separate or independent air force in April 1918 was an irrelevance to the army commanders and RFC staff engaged together in the ground campaign in France and would remain so even when the name was changed.

# 3

## *April Fools' Day 1918*

Today I find myself a Colonel RAF though I don't
feel particularly exhilarated by the thought.

*Richard Peirse, diary, 1 April 1918*[1]

There was a great deal of uncertainty on 1 April 1918 about
what the change to a separate air service might entail. It was
not only April Fools' Day but an Easter Monday. The young
RNAS officer, Richard Peirse, later to serve as Commander-in-
Chief of Bomber Command in the early years of the Second
World War, found himself stationed at Dunkirk with the 65th
Wing when the changeover occurred. On Easter Day he dined
with No. 2 Squadron, soon to become the 202nd squadron RAF
following the decision that RNAS squadrons should be re-
numbered by adding 200 to their original designation. The men,
Peirse noted in his diary, 'had a large gathering to celebrate
the departing hours of the RNAS and a general rough-house
ensued after dinner'. Two days later he found himself attacking
'stacks of papers and new RAF procedures and manuals . . .'[2]

There were no fanfares or ceremonies to mark the day
when the RAF was born. The formal changeover was indi-
cated by the simple device of a new rubber stamp. 'Royal Air
Force' in a large rectangular box was affixed to operational

47

reports over 'Royal Flying Corps'. RNAS reports were also altered on the first day when squadron record books were signed 'Officer Commanding RAF' rather than simply 'Squadron Commander/Commanding Officer'.[3] The Air Council worried in March that the supply of rubber stamps sent to the RFC Middle East would not arrive in time. Making the RAF immediately visible was a detail that evidently mattered, but the changeover made little impact at first. The development of a new service, with its own doctrine, its own ethos, and its own material presence took a great deal longer.

The new force consisted of 25,000 officers and 140,000 men, most of them technicians, mechanics or drivers. Only 8 per cent of the new force actually flew.[4] The RNAS had 5,300 officers and 49,000 men in March 1918, though not all of them joined the RAF; the rest came from the RFC units stationed in Britain, France and Italy, and from the Middle East Brigade, which ran British air forces in East Africa, Egypt, Palestine, Mesopotamia and Salonika. The personnel were all transferred on a temporary arrangement, for a period not exceeding four years, because no decision had been made about the future of a postwar air force. All of those transferred had the right within three months to register their objection and to return to their original army or navy service 'without prejudice', though it is not clear how many did so during the war.[5] The RAF stationed in Britain was divided between five commands, each under an officer with the rank of major-general, each responsible for a number of RAF groups. The commands were based in London, Salisbury, Birmingham, York and Glasgow (the latter also responsible for Ireland); any units attached to the Grand Fleet remained, however, under control of the Royal Navy.[6] Although the new Air Ministry directly owned only one of the sites, the plan in April 1918 was to establish at least thirty permanent bases after the war, with a further sixty-six temporary bases for training purposes, lighter-than-air craft and kite balloons. 'Is this very excessive?' minuted one official, to which the reply came back that 'London will remain the prime object of attack' in any future war, and deserved effective air defence.[7]

These changes made little difference to the air forces engaged in fighting in the war zones. The RNAS units that were not deployed to help combat the German offensive continued anti-submarine patrols and long and exhausting oversea reconnaissance flights against an enemy that, as it would turn out, had no intention of bringing out the German fleet to face the Royal Navy after the indecisive battle of Jutland in 1916. The operational reports of squadrons detailed to fly on long sea patrols show little change across the period when they became RAF units. In contrast to the costly fighting going on in France, former RNAS squadrons were still finding little to do. No. 4 Squadron (No. 204 as an RAF unit) filed regular daily summaries with 'nothing to report'; it saw real action only in October 1918 when it was sent on line patrols in Belgium and France, bombing and machine-gunning the retreating Germans.[8] For other squadrons, the changeover meant flying south to join former RFC units in ground combat, or to assist with the 8th Brigade in its long-distance bombing campaign. The foreboding in the Royal Navy that the RNAS would be swallowed up by the former army air service was not entirely misplaced. The Admiralty complained in May to the Air Ministry that 'our fears as to the desirability of the transfer are being confirmed as time goes on', citing the reduction in naval representation on the Air Council, and the transfer of naval bombing squadrons to army service.[9] In July Beatty complained that naval aircraft and trained pilots for the Grand

Fleet were simply not being produced. Though he had been promised 100 of the new torpedo-carrying Sopwith aircraft by July, there were only three; instead of the thirty-six trained pilots, there was none. Beatty had initially approved the change to the air services, but this time he suspected that the independent Air Ministry was diverting aircraft to other uses and neglecting the essential needs of the navy.[10]

The army on the other hand played a major part in the new RAF, where the majority of officers and other ranks had been former army personnel. Ranks in the new air service were army ranks, which is why Richard Peirse found himself to be a colonel on 1 April, when he had been a Squadron Commander RNAS. In October 1918 the Air Ministry explored the possibility of calling the most senior RAF officer 'General-in-Chief', a title that the King himself then appropriated.[11] Until a new uniform was decided on, airmen wore army khaki. Former naval airmen with the fleet could keep their dark blue uniforms, but there was some confusion over whether those airmen would keep their naval rank, or adopt the new army nomenclature, as the land-based units had done. The army also supplied canteens for the RAF, as well as supplying clothing, quartering and rations for RAF units at home and in the field.[12] Above all, the urgent necessity of coping with the German offensive in the spring of 1918, and the subsequent drive to breach the German defensive 'Hindenburg Line' in the autumn, meant that the main priority of the Air Ministry and the Ministry of Munitions was to keep the army supplied with aircraft and pilots. Losses were exceptionally severe, averaging 670 aircraft a month (one third of the force on the Western Front), so that re-supplying army squadrons soaked up much more of the expanded aircraft programme than had been expected.[13] It was here over the trenches on the Western Front that the RAF effectively began its long career fighting side by side with the army and the anti-aircraft artillery in noisy, dangerous combination. In July 1918 RAF Air Mechanic Thomas Spencer witnessed one spectacular episode of the air war over the base of No. 65 Squadron:

> Last night was one of the worst nights I have seen out here, Jerry came over at about 6,000 ft, the searchlights got him at once & the guns opened out. Twenty batteries banging shells at him at once, the air was full of shells, shrapnel, & the noise deafening to add to the row, he dropped 4 bombs & then loosed the remainder all at once, about 16 of them, you cannot imagine what it was like, the earth shook, the shells bursting & the bombs exploding & threw off dense clouds of black smoke, the noise was terrific . . . so Jerry got away . . . so ended one of the most thrilling airfights I have seen.[14]

By October 1918 the army on the Western Front had eighty-four squadrons in direct support, four on the Italian front, and thirteen in the Middle East Brigade, more than half of all the new RAF units.[15] If the sixty-four squadrons working with the navy in fleet support and anti-submarine patrols are added in, an overwhelming proportion of the separate air force was engaged as before on auxiliary operations for the navy and army.

Such a situation was predictable in the midst of a major war in which aircraft serving naval and military needs were already an established fact. But it placed into question exactly what the RAF had been formed for in the first place. The months following 1 April were spent trying to establish a clearer identity for the new service. The most urgent requirement was to find a settled leadership following Trenchard's decision to resign and Rothermere's own hesitation over whether to continue in an office in which his role was increasingly uncomfortable. The news of Trenchard's decision was published in mid-April after Rothermere had told Trenchard on 10 April that the War Cabinet had approved it. Rothermere's formal letter accepting the resignation was a deliberately harsh indictment of a man he found 'perfectly impossible'.[16] 'I cannot say I do so with any particular reluctance,' he wrote to Trenchard. ' . . . I believe your act in resigning your post as Chief of the Air Staff twelve days before myself and the large staff here were going into action to accomplish the gigantic task of the fusion of the Royal Naval Air Service and the Royal Flying Corps is an unparalleled incident in the public life of this country'.[17] The shock of Trenchard's impending departure had prompted Lloyd George to summon Smuts once again to review the crisis between the minister and the chief-of-staff, but Smuts, who had first-hand experience of Trenchard in action on the Air Policy Committee in 1917, recommended that he should be allowed to go. On the same day that Rothermere accepted the resignation, Smuts wrote to Lloyd George recommending as the best man for the job Frederick Sykes, Trenchard's nemesis.[18] Sykes arrived at the Hotel Cecil to take over; Trenchard cleared his desk and walked silently out of the building to temporary unemployment.

The crisis did not abate with the appointment of Sykes. He accepted the post despite his reluctance to abandon entirely his new role as an adviser at Versailles to the Allied Supreme War Council in favour, as he wrote in his memoirs, of 'the vortex of the Hotel Cecil'. He thought his task 'formidable', not least because the army and navy still saw air power as auxiliary and not as a third service 'with widespread functions of its own'.[19] He was more at home in a ministry than Trenchard, though he too thought that the ministerial officials were too many and their efficiency as a result too low – 'the repository for discarded members of other Ministries and the happy hunting ground of the careerist'.[20] Sykes was able to avoid too much time in the Hotel Cecil because he retained his role at Versailles, dividing his time between the two. But less than a week after his appointment, the vice-president of the Air Council, Lt.-General David Henderson, resigned on the grounds that it was not in the interest of the air service for him to work with someone he had disliked and distrusted since the beginning of the war, citing the 'atmosphere of intrigue and falsehood' that now permeated the ministry as one of his reasons for leaving. He left Rothermere and Smuts with his 'very unfavourable opinion' of the new chief-of-staff.[21]

The resignation of two men widely regarded as the architects of the army air service hinted to the public of a deeper crisis in the newly founded RAF. Some pointed the finger of blame at Lord Rothermere, who had already considered his own resignation on grounds of ill-health and his personal devastation at the death in February of his eldest son from wounds sustained in action. He had told Trenchard as much in their discussions in March. Trenchard later recalled that his first reaction had been 'Thank God', but his second a more cautious 'Is this true? I don't trust you to resign.'[22] Rothermere himself did hesitate over inflicting what would be a third blow to the infant service, but in the end the rumours and criticism circulating over the loss of Trenchard and Henderson pushed him to the final decision, and on 25 April 1918 his resignation was announced. In a letter to Lloyd George, Rothermere admitted he was 'suffering much from ill-health and insomnia' brought on, according to his friend Lord Beaverbrook, by the stress of overwork and trying to master his private grief.[23] Rothermere had not been popular with career airmen. Salmond complained in a letter to his parents in April about the 'arch blighter' in charge of the Ministry. 'His point of view,' Salmond continued, 'is no good for a soldier.'[24]

The third resignation prompted a flurry of speculation about what malaise lay at the heart of the new ministry. Beaverbrook judged that Rothermere 'was not the man to grapple with a political crisis', brought on it seemed by renewed tension between the military and the politicians. Lloyd George suspected that the resignations of Trenchard and Henderson were linked in some way to a broader conspiracy by senior military figures to undermine the government. He speculated that a cabal consisting of Trenchard, Haig, Lord Jellicoe and General William Robertson, recently replaced at the War Office, was orchestrating a showdown with his administration, but there was little or no substance to the charge. The government survived the debate on Rothermere's resignation in both houses. Lloyd George chose as Rothermere's successor a more neutral appointment.[25] On 27 April, Sir William Weir, the director of aeronautical production in the Ministry of Munitions and a member of the Air Council, was offered the post. His condition for acceptance was to be granted a peerage, because he felt ill-at-ease at the prospect of facing the tough debating techniques of the Commons. The King reluctantly agreed to yet further wartime ennoblement and he was created Lord Weir of Eastwood. He was a more rational choice than Rothermere, partly because he had no political experience or familiarity with the intrigues and posturing that had governed the creation and establishment of the ministry, partly because in his role at the Ministry of Munitions he had displayed a clear grasp of the needs of a modern air force and had succeeded in overcoming the prolonged feud between army and navy over production priorities. Weir was also a knowledgeable enthusiast for aviation, rather than an amateur.[26] The appointment of Weir, with Sykes as his chief-of-staff, stabilized the political crisis that surrounded the creation of the RAF and brought to office two men who were committed to making a single air service work.

For those airmen keen to establish a distinctive branch of the armed forces, there had to be clear material differences between the RAF and the other services. The most conspicuous way in which service identity could be established was to have a uniform that set the air force apart. The short period of time in which the new force had to be prepared, and the pressing issues of pay, discipline and administration that the Air Council had had to deal with before April, meant that the creation of a new uniform was still not settled by the time the RAF was inaugurated. A modified version of army uniform was introduced first, but it proved unpopular, undermining, according to the Air Council minutes, the new 'esprit de corps' that the air force needed. The new commander of RAF North-West reported 'evil effects' on the men who had to wear what was essentially still army dress.[27] A light blue uniform with much gold braid was the preferred option, and was finally approved in late May, and given royal sanction on 21 June, but there was a shortage of the necessary blue cloth. This, too, was not popular with the force. It was the kind of uniform, recalled John Slessor, 'which brought irresistibly to mind a vision of the gentleman who stands outside the cinema'. The sky-blue 'Ruritanian' costumes, as another RAF officer later put it, remained at first a rarity.[28] It was agreed that, in the field, RAF personnel could still wear khaki; officers who could not afford to pay for the new blue dress were permitted to continue to wear khaki uniform until it wore out, with the result that the RAF looked a motley force throughout 1918.[29] In the Middle East and India, it was recommended that khaki be worn in the hot season, and the blue uniform when it grew colder. Only by November did it prove possible to supply an adequate number of blue uniforms and to suspend the wearing of khaki by officers, except for overcoats. They were permitted to wear the dark blue naval overcoat or the army khaki coat until October 1919.[30] By this time the negative attitude towards sky blue and gold had had its effect. A darker grey-blue cloth was found, first for work uniforms then, on 15 September 1919, for all RAF dress. Non-officer ranks had to wait until 1921 before they were all able to wear grey-blue because of the large quantity of khaki still held in RAF stores.[31]

The search for a distinctive flag for the RAF proved even more difficult, provoking a long-running feud with the Admiralty. The Air Ministry proposed in May using either a white ensign without the red St George's Cross (to distinguish it from the principal flag of the Royal Navy) or a pale blue ensign, which better matched the new uniforms. The Admiralty immediately rejected the idea of a 'mutilated white ensign', or an ensign in red or blue. The naval view was that ensigns belonged only to the Royal Navy, 'by virtue of their origin and of long association', and asked the RAF to use the Union Jack flag with some appropriate emblem in the middle.[32] In July, Weir tried again to persuade the Admiralty to allow a white ensign for the RAF but was told by the First Lord that it was against the Defence of the Realm Act to fly an ensign on land without Admiralty permission, which would not be given. The Air Ministry persevered nevertheless and proposed in October to submit to the King a white ensign design or a Union Jack with an RAF badge superimposed, only to be told that the Union Jack violated Board of Trade regulations. When the white ensign was again proposed to the naval authorities as the RAF preference, the Admiralty remained utterly opposed to the idea that an ensign design could be appropriated by another service. The Air Ministry sought legal advice, to be told that the Admiralty's stubborn defence of the ensign was covered by Orders in Council from 1864, giving the Royal Navy exclusive right to use it.[33] When the navy found that two RAF stations had been observed already flying an ensign, the Air Council was told to have them removed at once.[34] There followed a long lull while the RAF focused on more serious issues for its peacetime survival, but in June 1920 the Admiralty was informed that a blue ensign had finally been selected, with the distinctive RAF red, white and blue roundel (first used as a recognition symbol on RAF aircraft in 1915 and known then as the 'target'), set on the pale blue background. The roundel was chosen, it was claimed, to honour the RAF dead; the small Union flag in the corner of the ensign to show it was a British service. The navy objected once again to a flag too close in design to the naval ensigns, and consulted the College of Heralds, responsible for authorizing flags and coats of arms, which confirmed that no flag could be approved which contained two different shades of the same colour, in this case light and dark blue. The Board of Admiralty prepared at once to inform the King, but their sense of triumph was short-lived. The RAF hurried to get to the monarch first. George V liked the new flag and approved it without demur, after more than two years of Air Ministry efforts.[35]

Another distinctive feature was the introduction of a women's component of the RAF, to supply auxiliary staff for air stations and air force administration, as well as women who could train as fitters and drivers to release men for active service, and who would owe their allegiance to the new force. The navy and the army had already organized a women's branch, and some of them now served with the RFC and the RNAS. The proposal was raised early in 1918 and the title 'Women's Royal Air Force' (WRAF) finally approved on 5 March and activated on 1 April, drawing 9,000 women from the existing army and navy women's services on a voluntary basis. The Director of Manning, Lt.-Colonel W. Bersey, was insistent that 'no pressure of any kind is to be used', for reasons that remain obscure.[36] The WRAF was from the start divided between women regarded as 'immobiles' and those regarded as mobile. Since accommodation was difficult to find – a situation made more complicated by the insistence that women should not be housed in proximity to men – preference was given to 'immobiles' who lived no more than three miles from an air station and could reach air stations by bus or rail. Mobile women were generally posted to France after initial training, where they worked in a range of clerical and auxiliary roles in a male-dominated world. The list of possible posts for women included familiar female jobs such as typist, cook, waitress and laundress, but also fifteen technical trades, from acetylene welder to tinsmith. The requirement for a 'Vegetable Woman' and a 'By-Product Woman' must have been understood at the time by the manning department, even if their function today is less obvious. Women also had the right to drive light vehicles of all kinds, but under no circumstances to drive a heavy tender.[37]

Lady Gertrude Crawford was recruited as the first Chief Superintendent of the WRAF, but she too joined the list of senior figures who left in April when it was decided that she should be replaced by a well-respected civil servant, working as a National Insurance Commissioner in Wales, Violet Douglas-Pennant. Her claim to fame was to have equipped a hospital with 500 beds in a single day during the first week of the war. She took the post in June 1918 with some reluctance following an exploratory month, and set about trying to create a better organization for a service where there were no effective welfare or health facilities and too few officers to run the corps – seventy-three in charge of 16,000 recruits at 500 air stations.[38] She contemplated resigning almost at once because she found the whole establishment 'hopelessly bad', but was persuaded again that she was witnessing the teething troubles of a new service and should persevere.[39] What followed remains open to dispute. After ten weeks in office she was brusquely dismissed without explanation by the recently appointed RAF Master of Personnel, Brigadier-General Sefton Brancker, her dismissal confirmed when she met Lord Weir a few days later. Weir reacted to pressure from the Minister of National Service, who threatened to stop allocating personnel to the WRAF because of allegations that it was failing to function effectively under a commander regarded as 'grossly unpopular'. The allegations, it was discovered, had been brought by a former clerk in a Newcastle toy shop, Katherine Andrew, who had been denied promotion in the newly created WRAF, resigned in protest and denounced Douglas-Pennant to Weir as a 'disreputable woman'. The Air Minister insisted on his right to dismiss officers who undermined the service (although it would have been surprising if the officer had been a man), and refused to reinstate her. Weir was convinced that she had been a mistaken appointment and that the problems facing the WRAF were largely her responsibility.[40] Her successor was Helen Gwynne-Vaughan, the controller of the Women's Army Auxiliary Corps in France, who coped more effectively than her predecessor but who prudently refused to reinstate Katherine Andrew to the service.

Douglas-Pennant did not go quietly. The interview with Brancker, who had just arrived back from the United States to take up his post as Master of Personnel, was a travesty of procedure. An officer relieved of his or her position was entitled to a period of notice and a detailed report justifying the decision. Brancker told her to leave on the day of the interview without a proper explanation. When he tried to shake her hand at the end of their brief exchange, she justifiably refused, though Brancker saw this as some evidence that the rumours about her personality might be correct.[41] In early September 1918 Douglas-Pennant requested a full enquiry into her dismissal, which Lloyd George refused. Her case rested on the obstruction she had found from the men running the stations and the manning directorate, who disliked taking orders from a woman. Bersey, whose role it was to oversee manning in general, insisted that Douglas-Pennant would always have to go through his office rather than communicate directly with the male commanding officers at air force stations. The conditions in the camps, she told Churchill in February 1919, were 'extremely bad, in some cases scandalous', but the men held her attempts at reform at arm's length.[42] Her chief drawback was her completely civilian background and lack of experience. An attractive and energetic woman, she saw herself, with evident justification, as the victim of male prejudice. Her case continued to attract support into the 1920s, with enquiries set up by the House of Lords, but not until the 1930s was she finally exonerated. The birth of the WRAF, like its parent service, was surrounded by an unanticipated level of intrigue and argument.

The real issue of identity for the RAF was not to be found in uniforms or flags, or in the more trivial efforts to establish difference by adopting a unique form of saluting, or the formation of RAF bands (both of which occupied valuable Air Council time in 1918). The critical test for all those who had argued the case for a separate service was to establish a body of air doctrine that made the contribution of air power strategically distinct from the functions of army and navy. A particular air strategy had been anticipated in the political efforts to establish a ministry and the new air force. Both air defence of the United Kingdom and long-range bombing of Germany were ideas cemented in Smuts' two reports in the summer of 1917, and both were used after April 1918 to demonstrate that the RAF was more than an auxiliary prop for the established services. Nevertheless, the RAF began its new career with doctrine that was borrowed from the RFC and RNAS in their auxiliary role. One of Rothermere's many complaints about Trenchard was his apparent failure to produce a coherent strategy for the new air force in his three months as chief-of-staff. In reality, the problem was not that Trenchard lacked a strategy, simply that it was a strategy tied to the offensive use of aircraft in support of the army or, in Sykes's uncharitable view, 'battering-ram tactics'.[43] Trenchard's ideas were closely reflected in the army General Staff pamphlet 'Fighting in the Air', republished in April 1918 from its March 1917 edition. The priority was to achieve 'ascendancy in the air' against the enemy air force: 'To seek out and destroy the enemy's forces must therefore be the guiding principle of our tactics in the air.'[44] For the air units supporting the army, active counter-force patrols were to be combined with direct ground support using bombs and machine-guns against enemy troops, billets and transport, and longer range bombing of communications and production facilities. Those attacks on rear areas deemed most useful 'were in connection with operations on the ground'.[45] Defensive aviation, on the other hand, was not regarded as useful either at the fighting front or at home. 'In the air even more than on the ground', concluded another General Staff study, 'the true defence lies in attack . . .'[46] Squadron record books describe day after day of 'Offensive Patrols' or 'Patrolled Army Front', sometimes achieving little more than scaring German aircraft back to base, sometimes engaging in 'indecisive combats', only occasionally recording an enemy aircraft shot down or the loss of comrades in action ('Lt. White last seen over Grillancourt 8.45 p.m.').[47] The air war, like the ground campaign, was a slow war of attrition, less thrilling and more mundane than the popular image of aerial combat.

One of Sykes's first tasks as chief-of-staff was to strengthen the air and anti-air defences around London and what he called 'other nerve centres'. By June 1918 there were 469 anti-aircraft guns (in comparison with a handful in 1915) and 622 searchlights, manned by 6,000 officers and men, together with 6th Brigade RAF, which comprised 376 aircraft (166 serviceable), 660 officers and 3,500 other ranks. Squadrons based in north-east France and Belgium were also detailed to try to intercept German bombers on their approach or return. The RAF now had available a trio of effective fighter aircraft: the Bristol F.2B, the Royal Aircraft Factory's S.E.5a and the Sopwith F.1 Camel. The extensive and improved resources available may well have discouraged further German incursions. The last raid was on 19 May 1918, when seven from the small number of Gotha bombers available to German air forces were lost, six to guns and fighters, one to accident – 25 per cent of the attacking force.[48] The enlarged air defence system may have given the RAF an independent strategic function, but until 1940 it was never properly tested. More significant at the time and for the future development of the RAF was what Sykes called in his memoirs his 'cherished project' for the strategic bombing of the German homeland. While it is true that Sykes put much of his energy as chief-of-staff into establishing a bomber force that was not tied to control by the army on the ground, there was nothing original about his strategy. Long-range bombing of the German industrial cities within aircraft range had been mooted for several years, and detailed plans developed. The stumbling block to initiating a campaign was the short range of British bomber aircraft and the remorseless demand for air equipment generated by the land battle.

The evolution of a practical bombing strategy in fact owed little to Sykes. Both Smuts and his chief adviser, David Henderson, favoured bombing the German homeland and pressed this as a possibility in the summer of 1917. By the autumn of that year the RNAS too had a coherent programme for what would later be called 'strategic bombing'. In September 1917 Lt.-Commander Lord Tiverton (later Viscount Halsbury) sent to the Air Board a 'Scheme for bombing German Industrial centres' that defined four groups of probable targets: the Düsseldorf group, Cologne group, Mannheim group and the Saar Valley. Bombing the Ruhr–Rhineland area was regarded as the priority, because a large proportion of German iron, steel, coal and engineering production was concentrated there. Tiverton and his colleagues in the RNAS analysed the kind of aircraft needed, the scale of the force, the probable bomb loads required, the differences between night and day operations and the material and moral impact of bomb destruction.[49] The Director of Flying Operations added a detailed list of objectives in order of importance: Grade C comprised the capital cities of the Central Powers (Berlin, Vienna, Sofia and Constantinople); Grade B included German communications;

objectives given the top Grade A included the major industrial sectors, chemicals, iron and steel, aero-engine and magneto works, submarine bases and shipbuilding yards, gun shops and engine repair depots.[50] The War Trade Intelligence Department of the Admiralty supplied Tiverton and his RNAS colleagues with detailed target information to be used when bombing became a technical possibility.

The RNAS preparations for bombing contributed to the operational planning for the 41st Wing established in October 1917 on the instructions of the War Cabinet to undertake bombing of the Saarland area. Trenchard, despite his reservations about the practical difficulties of achieving very much in winter weather with a tiny force, did see long-distance bombing as one way of wearing down the German war machine to make the task at the front easier. In October 1917 his memorandum on 'Future Air Organisation' suggested that thirty squadrons would be needed in 1918 for bombing German manufacturing centres if there were to be any serious effect on munitions output and 'sufficient effect on the inhabitants to destroy their confidence and break down their morale'.[51] The 'moral impact' of bombing has long been associated with Trenchard's postwar strategy for the RAF, but its roots can be found in his wartime writing. In November 1917 he returned to the theme that the moral impact of bombing was likely to be considerably greater than the material results, but this could only be achieved with better bombers capable of reaching targets deeper inside Germany 'in order to secure the all important moral results of bombing purely German towns' and creating what he called a 'sustained anxiety'.[52]

Sykes was fortunate that he came to office just as a new generation of heavy bombers was made available. The Handley Page O/400 entered service in April 1918. Britain's largest wartime aircraft, with a 100-foot wingspan, the bomber was capable of carrying up to 2,000 pounds of bombs and utilized a newly developed Mk1A bombsight to increase accuracy. During the time Sykes was chief-of-staff 400 were produced, with a further 170 manufactured under licence in the United States. The bomber began its operational career supporting the British army as it tried to stem the German March Offensive, but by the summer was available for long-range operations into Germany. Sykes was also fortunate that in Lord Weir he found a firm advocate of attacks on the German home front using a force deliberately set aside from the 'Surplus Air Fleet' that Weir had hoped to create for 1918. On 14 May 1918, two weeks after assuming office as Air Minister, Weir provided the War Cabinet with what he regarded as his inaugural statement of intent: a rapid development of aerial strength devoted to the weakening of German civilian morale and the interruption of the German industrial effort. Weir thought it not unrealistic that bombing would contribute materially 'towards bringing about a definite demand for peace' from the German enemy.[53] Sykes himself finally gave shape to his own thoughts on the role of an independent RAF in June 1918 when he submitted to the War Cabinet a long statement on air strategy in which he suggested that air power was capable of transforming the way the war, and future wars, would be fought. Modern war, Sykes argued, was now a war of 'national attrition', and the best way for the new RAF to contribute to that process was to engage in long-range offensives against the 'root industries' of the German war effort, and 'to break down the moral [sic] of his nation'. The 'wholesale bombing of densely populated industrial centres', he continued, 'would go far to destroy the morale of the operatives', an early iteration of what would later be called 'area bombing'.[54]

The search for a clear strategic identity for the RAF resulted in May 1918 in the creation of the so-called 'Independent Force' for the long-range bombing of German targets. On 13 May the Air Council was given approval by the Supreme War Council to undertake a long-distance bombing programme, and the following day the Army Council was informed that a new Independent Air Force was to be set up under the direct control of the Air Ministry, not the British Expeditionary Force, the first clear statement of the separate status the RAF had gained in April.[55] This was a solution neither Haig nor the French high command liked very much, since support for the struggle on the Western Front was paramount, while French leaders worried that German aircraft would retaliate against French industrial centres. The War Cabinet was also unenthusiastic about the idea that the Air Ministry should control any air forces, but it allowed the new formation to go ahead on a provisional basis. The new force was in effect a military-political instrument designed by Weir and Sykes to demonstrate that air power could be exercised separately from the activity of the army and navy and thus justify the creation of both the Air Ministry and the RAF.

There remained the issue of who would command the independent element. To Sykes' discomfiture, Weir decided to offer the post to Trenchard, despite his private disapproval of Trenchard's 'very indefinite reasons' for resigning.[56] The former chief-of-staff was not an obvious choice given his view that the needs of the army came first, and his sceptical judgement about the adequacy of existing bomber forces. Nor did Trenchard accept the post easily. On 14 April, the day of his formal resignation, he had applied to the War Office for permission to return to an army career with his former regiment, in charge of a battalion of infantry. Rothermere supported the application, no doubt relieved to see Trenchard at a safe distance. But the War Office turned down the application, perhaps because Trenchard was too conspicuous and contentious a figure to be given junior command. He was offered instead command of a division, but Trenchard thought he lacked the experience.[57] Haig was keen to have him back in some capacity or other but offered nothing concrete. On 1 May, the day Weir began in office, Trenchard wrote to assure the new minister that he wanted to help the RAF 'to the utmost of my power' and suggested that he might be a General Officer Commanding of the whole RAF with a seat on the Air Council, giving advice on policy and touring the RAF stations overseas. This was a strange request, not only because it would pit him face-to-face with Sykes, but because he had resigned only weeks before from a very similar post. Not surprisingly Weir refused and instead offered Trenchard a choice of one of four roles: Inspector General of the RAF overseas; Inspector General of the RAF at home; RAF Commander-in-Chief Middle East or Commander of the Independent Force in France. Trenchard havered on them all. The role of Inspector General he thought would give him no responsibility and no power of command. He remained doubtful that independent bombing would achieve very much and, like Smuts in 1917, saw the Middle East as a military dead end. On 6 May Weir lost patience and told him to choose one or have nothing. For two days Trenchard continued to dither, and his final decision to accept command of the new bomber force on 8 May was done with scarcely concealed reluctance: 'I have already stated my objections several times, and which I think will lead to efficiency being lowered. But since you are set on it and need a commander, I will accept.'[58]

On 13 May the Air Council notified Trenchard that he was

now General Officer Commanding the Independent Force, and charged him with the task of attacking German industrial targets of military importance, though no mention was made of the expected moral effects on the workforce. On 24 May the War Cabinet accepted the decision to inaugurate the new force with Trenchard in charge.[59] On the way to his new command based around Nancy, where the 41st Wing operated, Trenchard stopped at RAF headquarters where, he observed, 'everyone seemed opposed to the formation of the Independent Force', much as he had been.[60] He arrived in Nancy on 20 May, and assumed command on 5 June; on 15 June the transfer from control by Haig and the BEF to control by the Air Ministry was completed.[61] The force he found was anything but a flagship for the RAF. There were four squadrons available, their operations divided between assistance for the army and the bombing of the Saarland when weather permitted. The force was supposed to grow to twenty-four squadrons by October, well below the figure of sixty-six squadrons for long-range bombing that Haig had requested the previous November. The slower expansion of output in 1918 and high losses at the front compromised even the more modest figure of twenty-four. In June, the force had five squadrons, by August seven and at the end of the war in November only ten, one of which consisted of fighters.[62] This was not the force that Trenchard had been expecting to command. In an interview many years later he complained that the 'high-sounding name' of the Independent Force was so much moonshine: 'What I commanded was a few squadrons. I was not anybody very much.'[63]

Shortly after his assumption of command, Trenchard sent a report to the Inter-Allied Aviation Committee at Versailles to explain what he saw as his role. Aircraft could only be diverted to long-range bombing, he argued, once German aviation was defeated. Once air superiority was established then surplus machines would be freed 'for fighting the Germans in GERMANY'.[64] A counter-force offensive was, in Trenchard's view, a critical factor if bombing were to succeed at all. The plans he laid down for 1919, had the war continued, divided the operations of the Independent Force equally between attacks on enemy aerodromes and long-range attacks against industrial targets.[65] This was sound advice, given what is now known about all bombing offensives, but it was not what Weir and Sykes had had in mind. Trenchard allowed his small force to be diverted to attacking the German air force and German communications to the front, turning it into a force that appeared to be part auxiliary, part separate. This diversion was evident from the regular operational résumés sent to the Air Ministry from Trenchard's headquarters. On 8/9 July the force dropped five tons of bombs, by day on the aerodrome at Bühl and railway sidings at Luxembourg, by night on aerodromes at Boulay and Freisdorf and on two trains. On 19/20 July, bombs were dropped on the munitions works at Oberndorf by day, and at night on aerodromes at Freisdorf, Boulay and Morhange, trains near Saarbrücken and Rémilly, and three industrial plants in Mannheim. On 12/13 September, six tons were dropped on Courcelles, Orny and Verny rail junctions, and railways at Metz (using four of the squadrons).[66] That month, Brigadier-General Percy Groves, director of operations in the Air Ministry, complained to Sykes that in defiance of RAF policy, Trenchard's campaign 'amounts to the diversion of maximum effort against targets of subsidiary importance.'[67] However, the pattern of operations remained the same down to the armistice in November. Once again in command, Trenchard followed his own strategic instincts.

Bombing at long distance was a difficult and risky operation in the conditions of 1918. Bombing by night presented a severe challenge once German blackout regulations were in place. Bomber aircraft dropped clusters of parachute flares which illuminated an area up to a quarter of a square mile, but they carried the risk that the wind would float them away. It was calculated that one third of aircraft failed to find the designated objective at night (and 18 per cent by day).[68] Bomb-aiming was still a primitive skill, even with an improved bombsight. Flying at between 10,000 and 15,000 feet, close observation of the target and of the results of bombing was difficult; it was later found that one third of the bombs failed to explode.[69] The weather played a major part in limiting operations or in increasing the risks pilots faced as they tried to operate through cloud or high wind. In October 1918, mist, fog and low cloud meant that on nineteen days and twenty-two nights no operations were possible at all.[70] Even when flying was possible, technical problems could force aircraft to return to base or attempt an improvised landing. In a raid on Thionville station on 6 June, six out of eleven DH.9 bombers had to return with engine trouble. Losses due to non-combat damage were high, usually higher than losses to the enemy. In August 1918, when the weather allowed 100 tons to be dropped on enemy targets, fifty-four machines were wrecked and written off. Aircraft missing, either to crashes or enemy action, totalled twenty-seven.[71]

Enemy aircraft were nevertheless an ever-present menace, which is why suppressing the German air forces was Trenchard's priority. As the bombing became a regular feature, so the German high command moved to establish proper air defences, as the British had done. By 1918 there was a network of 400 searchlights and 1,200 anti-aircraft guns, and a number of nighttime decoy targets, illuminated amidst the blackout. An Air Warning Service was established, using a combination

of ground and aerial observation.[72] Aircraft were diverted from
the front, and by August 1918 there were sixteen home defence
squadrons of Albatross, Fokker and Pfalz fighters, a total of
240 planes. They were supported by at least ninety aircraft
stationed on the Alsace-Lorraine front which, like the RAF units
based in Belgium to cut off German bomber raids, tried to
intercept the bombers on their way to their more distant targets.[73] The RAF bombers flew in close formation, usually in
groups of six. When possible they would have an escort of
fighters by day. German aircraft attacked when they could in
large numbers, to inflict heavy losses, but they also hunted in
smaller groups to pick off any stragglers from a bomber formation. Success was sometimes almost total. On 31 July 1918, a
force of nine DH.9s was attacked by forty single-seat fighters
and all but two destroyed; on 26 September, seven bombers
were attacked by a larger fighter force and only one returned
with a wounded pilot and a dead observer.[74] In turn, casualties
could be imposed on the German enemy either by escorting
fighters or by the machine-guns of the bomber formation. In
August 1918, the Independent Force claimed nineteen enemy
aircraft shot down, but this was scant compensation for the
overall loss that month of eighty-one of the small force
available.

Sykes was unperturbed by the difficulties and the small
scale. His aim was to expand the Independent Force into an
Inter-Allied Air Force using French, Italian and United States
bomber units alongside those of the RAF.[75] The anxiety of the
French high command that bombing long-distance would di-
vert effort away from the front line was heightened by June,
when it was evident that the German army on the Western
Front was facing crisis and might crack under continued pressure. Sykes tried to persuade the Inter-Allied Aviation

Committee in late May that an Allied force would have more impact on the German home front than the RAF operating alone, but the French remained unconvinced, although a meeting in early June face-to-face with Georges Clemenceau, French President of the Supreme War Council, did elicit for Sykes what he described as a 'hearty endorsement' from the French leader.[76] In August Weir wrote to Clemenceau explaining that long-distance bombing was not merely in a narrow sense military, it was also political, being 'an attack on the morale of the industrial population with the object of reducing output and of producing a tendency towards peace'.[77] The French high command might well have asked for the recall of the Independent Force, because it operated outside the overall command structure, led by the French Marshal Ferdinand Foch, who was unenthusiastic about strategic bombing and hostile to Trenchard.[78] The Independent Force survived largely because it was an increasing irrelevance once Allied efforts were devoted to exploiting the optimistic prospects on the Western Front against a crumbling enemy. To prevent French leaders from insisting on terminating the RAF experiment, Weir and Sykes agreed that overall control of the Independent Force should pass to Foch, who could use its resources in any emergency in the ground war.[79] Only in October did the French leaders agree that an Inter-Allied Independent Air Force could be created, and on 26 October Trenchard was notified that he would be its commander. The decision was overtaken by events, for within three weeks the Germans had sued for an armistice.[80]

The plans to develop an Inter-Allied force highlighted the growing collaboration between the RAF and the American Air Service, established in Europe since the United States declaration of war in 1917. American and Canadian volunteers were already a feature of the RFC. A group of 210 United States university students came to train in Britain to join the RFC, and 115 of them became casualties.[81] During the war 1,239 Canadian air officers and 2,750 other ranks were seconded to the RFC, RNAS and RAF; with Canadian volunteers, the total number who served was 8,000. In August 1918 a separate Canadian flying corps was finally established.[82] The new United States Air Service was attached to the American Army expeditionary force in Europe. The overall commander, General John Pershing, shared the view of Haig and Trenchard that offensive operations in support of the ground armies was the best use of America's still very limited air resources. Even American air officers keen on bombing as a distinct strategy still saw the operations as essentially raids on tactical targets behind the front to assist the army.[83] Two officers, Major Raymond Bolling and Lt.-Colonel Edgar Gorrell, were more committed to the maximum view that air power might yet prove decisive. Bolling headed the American Air Mission to Europe in June 1917, where he discussed air strategy with British airmen; Gorrell was made Chief of the Strategical Section in November 1917. The Bolling mission recommended 260 American squadrons by 1919, including sixty dedicated to long-range bombing.[84] In summer 1918, Gorrell increased the planned scale to 358 squadrons, 110 of them for bombing, and the War Department authorized the plan in June. Production was planned for 17,500 bomber aircraft, to be produced in the United States from British and Italian designs, but by the time of the Armistice only sixty bombers had reached the front. Those American aircraft that did make it to France served like the RAF, chiefly in close support of the ground army.[85]

The balance-sheet showing the achievements of the 'independent' elements of the RAF in the months of its wartime existence is unimpressive. The limited results help to explain why after the Armistice the new service faced such strong political and military pressure to terminate what many regarded as a purely temporary, wartime expedient. It is worth observing that the Royal Navy's hostility to the RAF and defence of the established role of the RNAS was scarcely justified by what air-sea aviation achieved during the war. Research showed that Royal Navy aircraft sank only three small German vessels: one torpedo boat, one tug (which was raised and repaired) and one small harbour boat. Not a single German merchant vessel was sunk, while three small Turkish ships were torpedoed, with unverified results; only two German submarines, U32 and U59 (the latter bombed in a dry dock), were in fact destroyed by seaplanes, although the RNAS claimed during the war to have sunk 100.[86] There were throughout the war only twenty-nine combined sea-air operations in the North Sea; in 47 per cent of cases seaplanes were unable to take off from the water, and out of twelve aeroplanes used, three failed to take off from ship decks and five were lost at sea. [87] The use of aircraft at sea was most successful in the role of observation and reconnaissance, in forcing submarines to submerge, and in bombing enemy ports and naval installations, but the days when air-sea warfare could be based around high-performance aircraft carriers and radar-directed operations were still far in the future.

Nonetheless, the achievements registered by the air defence and anti-aircraft structure set up during the war were every bit as modest. One postwar calculation showed that of the thirty-nine German raids recorded over the mainland in 1917–1918, only twenty-one were sighted at all by British aircraft; out of the 1,737 sorties by defensive aircraft, 1,592 (91.7 per cent) never saw the enemy.[88] Statistics compiled on the wartime casualties inflicted on enemy bombers were equally modest: thirteen aircraft were brought down by anti-aircraft fire, three by day, ten by night; nine were accounted for by British fighter aircraft, five by day, four by night. British losses amounted to two aircraft shot down by British anti-aircraft guns, five by enemy aircraft, and twelve written off when they crash landed.[89] The evidence of just how difficult it was to intercept enemy aircraft was later used by the army to justify returning the air force to army and navy control. Like the air war at sea, effective air defence depended on the advent of more advanced equipment and radar intelligence.

The greatest disappointment came from the performance of the Independent Force, on which Sykes and Weir had staked their claim to a separate air service. During the five months of its operational existence the Force dropped just 537 tons of bombs, 160 by day and 377 by night. Of this quantity, 220 tons were dropped on railway targets in support of the ground army and a roughly equal quantity on enemy air bases and air force installations. The tonnage dropped on targets more than eighty-five miles from the front line (a distance adopted by the RAF as a measure of long-range bombing) was just forty-seven tons.[90] Most of this tonnage fell on the German city and port of Mannheim-Ludwigshafen (twenty-four tons); some five tons were dropped on Koblenz, five tons on Frankfurt. Other cities hit with much smaller loads included Bonn, Cologne, Darmstadt, Düren, Stuttgart and Wiesbaden.[91] The whole bomb tonnage could be carried in the Second World War by a dozen Lancaster bombers. Over the course of 1918 the RFC/RAF dropped 321,000 bombs, but only an estimated 5,000 of this total were dropped by the Independent Force on German towns. The independent campaign contributed just 8 per cent of the total bomb tonnage dropped between 1915 and

1918 by British aircraft.[92] This result was dictated by the small size of the Independent Force, starved as it was of an adequate number of aircraft and personnel by the demands of the fighting fronts, but also by Trenchard's own preference for tactical rather than strategic targets. In November 1918 only ten out of ninety-nine squadrons in France and 140 out of 1,799 aircraft were allocated to Trenchard.[93] At the war's end he issued a communiqué for his force praising them for bombing Germany with such vigour that they assisted 'in bringing about the demoralization that has produced this Armistice'. His private view, consigned to his diary the same day, was more in keeping with his own ambivalence about an independent campaign: 'A more gigantic waste of effort and personnel there has never been in any war'.[94]

Postwar surveys of the damage done to German targets confirmed that the bombing had had little material effect. German officials found the bombing of railway communications 'annoying'; the directors of those blast furnaces subjected to raids insisted that the bombing was inaccurate and ineffective. The psychological impact on the bombed population, on the other hand, was regarded by German officials as substantial. In postwar interviews, the mayors of the bombed cities agreed that the moral effect had been 'very considerable'. Once casualties mounted, 'panic became general'. This had been one of the aims of the offensive. In August 1918 the Air Ministry, citing letters from home found on German prisoners, observed that the population in the bombed regions was apparently 'unsettled and terrified'. From this a conclusion was drawn that was to influence British bombing strategy down to the end of the Second World War: 'it is certain that the moral of the German population becomes lower as the range and power of our bombing squadrons increase'.[95] In his despatch on the work of the Independent Force, Trenchard famously enshrined this conclusion in RAF strategic culture when he claimed that 'at present the moral effect of bombing stands undoubtedly to the material effect in a proportion of 20 to 1 . . .', an assertion for which no firm quantitative evidence existed, or was likely to exist.[96]

The aerial assault on the war-willingness of the German population raised significant ethical issues about the violation of civilian immunity. The German bombing of British cities had provoked widespread outrage at an enemy regarded as manifestly criminal. 'The cowardly wickedness of such raids,' wrote one diarist in November 1917, 'is almost incredible; to think of defenceless, innocent women and children and old men and boys being ruthlessly murdered and mutilated by these devils in the air . . .'[97] Bombing of German cities could be interpreted as legally justified reprisal against a barbarous enemy, though the Air Staff was anxious that British raids should not be seen as a mere response in kind but instead 'as a definite war campaign', so Weir informed the War Cabinet in August 1918, worked out with 'elaborate preparations'.[98] There is little evidence that bombing to demoralize civilians was regarded as morally unacceptable or illegal either at the time or since, although the German mayors interviewed in 1919 did condemn the deliberate bombing of 'workmen's colonies' as a possible war crime. In his memoirs, Sykes was at pains to claim that British bombing was not an example of 'frightfulness' (the term widely used to describe terror bombing), but simply a reflection of the harsh reality that it is 'impossible to humanize modern warfare'.[99] Trenchard had no doubt that killing German civilians was part of his policy. In early November 1918 he explained to Salmond, RAF commander in France, that he preferred to use high explosive rather than incendiary bombs against German targets 'to create moral effect and to kill'.[100]

The bombing by both sides in the war technically violated the intention in the Hague Conventions of 1899 and 1907 that explosive projectiles from balloons, airships or any other flying vehicle should be prohibited, but the extent to which this had the force of international law was open to interpretation, since a final decision had been postponed until a third Hague Conference, which never materialized, and most of the major powers refused to ratify the bombing clause.[101] Article 25, which prohibited the bombardment by whatever means of undefended 'towns, villages, dwellings or buildings' was taken to apply to aircraft too, but this clause left open the awkward definition of what was meant by 'undefended'. This was a matter of judgement for armed forces, but the prevailing sentiment during the Hague discussions was that modern states would observe the generally accepted notions of civilized warfare. These were vague limitations, far from legally binding. When the Imperial General Staff called for a formal legal opinion on aerial bombing in April 1918, they were informed that since none of the enemy powers had ratified the Hague Convention of 1907, they could not expect their enemy to abide by international agreement. More significantly, France had failed to ratify either. In a coalition where one power had not signed international legal instruments, the allies were also released from their obligation.[102] This was so much legal sophistry, but it confirmed that RAF bombing of distant civilian targets could not be considered illegal. When in 1919 the British Committee of Enquiry into Breaches of the Laws of War considered whether German airmen should be arraigned for bombing British 'undefended towns', Trenchard himself told the War Cabinet that his force had done much the same. In October

1919, the War Cabinet decided not to pursue the principle that bombing was contrary to law.[103] Not until the Geneva Convention of 1949 were restrictions on bombing civilians and the civilian milieu first introduced. Despite initial government prohibition in the late 1930s and the first months of the Second World War, the RAF was to return to civilian targeting in the bomber offensive of the next war, and with broadly similar reasoning.

If the independent operations of the new RAF showed little evidence that a separate service had really been necessary, the triumphant end to the ground campaigns on the Western Front and in the Middle East underscored the extent to which British military aviation had come of age as a successful tactical air force. The pursuit of a beaten enemy gave the RAF the opportunity to demonstrate how important counter-force and ground support operations had become. In addition to suppressing German air forces, RAF aircraft bombed and strafed German troops on the move or in trenches, attacked transport columns and bombed incoming supplies and ammunition dumps. Statistics compiled for 1918 claimed that the RAF destroyed 12,000 enemy artillery batteries, destroyed 1,150 gun pits, took 256,000 reconnaissance photographs and fired 321,000 machine-gun rounds.[104] Reliable or not, the figures display a sense of the scale of RAF ground support operations that absorbed the activity of the great majority of the personnel. In the Middle East, RAF units hounded Ottoman forces in the final offensive through Palestine and Syria. Aircraft hovered around Turkish aerodromes, dropping a bomb every time there was a sign of movement, and machine-gunning the hangars at the end of each sortie. Troops on the ground were pursued by air attacks as they withdrew, and subjected to repeated bombing and strafing. Salmond's brother and RAF commander in the Middle East, Brigadier-General Geoffrey Salmond, sent a grim report back to the Air Ministry about the carnage his air force inflicted on the Turkish retreat: 'I have been all through these columns and I have never seen anything so appalling and sickening. Gun piled against gun, horses underneath mixed up with oxen, motor lorries abandoned without stopping the engine and running amok and then, finally, overturning, dead Turks, smells indescribable.'[105] Against a beaten enemy, the remorseless activity of the RAF contributed to the final victory on the ground more certainly than any independent campaign.

The day and night before the war ended, on 10/11 November 1918, the Independent Force was, ironically enough, engaged solely on army support operations. Nine tons of bombs were dropped on railway sidings at Ehrhange, on the Metz–Sablon railway, and on air bases at Morhange, Lellingen and Frescaty. The first of a new generation of heavy long-range bombers, the Handley Page V/1500, was ready but arrived too late for operations. Weir and Sykes had planned for a great offensive in 1919 against the German homeland, but the plan was overtaken by events. On the cusp of proving itself more than an auxiliary arm, the RAF, with its 22,647 aeroplanes and seaplanes and 198 squadrons, was still tied to its parent services. The birth of the RAF in April 1918 gave no guarantee that the infant would survive into peacetime adolescence.

# 4

# *'A Very Gruelling Business': Saving the RAF*

We contend that the British policy is to develop the independent
conception of the air as an art, as an arm, and as a service; and that
this method alone will secure that qualitative ascendancy and
superiority which the safety of the country requires . . .

*Winston Churchill, October 1921*[1]

In June 1933 Air Vice-Marshal Brooke-Popham gave the after-
dinner speech on 'The Spirit of the Air Force' at a special
event organized to celebrate twenty-one years of the Royal Air
Force. The date actually commemorated was the founding of
the Royal Flying Corps in 1912, but the RAF elided the two
organizations together as if there had been a continuous
history of an independent flying arm. Brooke-Popham's
remarks made evident that the naval air service was a historical
detour. The RFC-RAF lineage was paramount. Brooke-
Popham had wanted to mention famous names from the
wartime years but realized that they had almost all died in
combat and that this might give the air force an unnecessarily
morbid image. Nevertheless, dead or alive, the airmen contributed by their 'courage and determination' to creating the
soul of the RAF, which after twenty-one years Brooke-Popham
regarded as 'permanent and fundamental'.[2]

The speech marked a particular historic moment for the RAF, but Brooke-Popham's seamless narrative masked a very different reality. The RAF was created out of bitter arguments over its necessity, and for half a decade after 1918 the future of the RAF as an independent service, separate from the army and navy, hung by a thread. The principal advocate of an end to air power independence remained the Admiralty, which might explain the absence of the navy in Brooke-Popham's talk, but by 1921 the army too began to have grave doubts about whether it made strategic and budgetary sense to keep the RAF. This was a far cry from the optimistic expectations of the Air Staff when the war ended that the RAF ought to play an expanded role in the defence of the motherland and the Empire. On 9 December 1918, a month after the Armistice, Sykes drew up a memorandum for the Cabinet on 'Air Power Requirements of the Empire'. He urged the government not to demobilize the air force too rapidly, because specialized air forces were essential to the future security of Britain's imperial territories. Air power, he continued, had tremendous potential, so that in peace or in war 'the nation which thinks in three dimensions will lead those still thinking in two'.

What followed was a classic description of a strategy that has come to be known as 'Douhetism', after the Italian airman Giulio Douhet, who argued in his book *Il dominio dell'aria* (*The Command of the Air*), first published in 1921, that any future war ought to begin with an annihilating air strike against the enemy's cities and civilians as a swifter and ultimately more humane route to victory than the four costly years of attrition between 1914 and 1918.Sykes 'strategic considerations' anticipated Douhet by some years:

Future wars between civilized nations will be struggles for life in which entire populations, together with their industrial resources, will be thrown into the scale. Evolution has brought about the creation of air fleets to meet the demands of such warfare. These will consist of home defence units and striking forces. The objectives of striking forces will be nerve centres, the armies and navies of the opponent, the population as a whole, his national moral [sic] and the industries, without which he cannot wage war.[3]

In early January 1919 Sykes even initiated discussions with the Admiralty to get the navy's agreement that the achievement of 'Command of the Air' was the responsibility of the RAF, while command of the sea was the navy's business.[4] Although Sykes was to remain in office for only a few more weeks, the strategic principles he outlined at the end of the war came to dominate RAF strategic thinking down to the start of the next, without reference to Douhet. Home air defence and strategic bombing gave to the air force a unique strategic profile. Sykes recommended a peacetime establishment for the two strategic forces of thirty-seven squadrons, twenty for defence, seventeen as the air striking force. The addition of squadrons for air-sea cooperation, empire defence and support for the army brought the total recommended by Sykes to 154 squadrons, not far short of the number at the end of the war.[5]

Sykes was to be swiftly disillusioned about the possibility of maintaining a substantial air element at the heart of British strategy. By 1920, the whole RAF consisted of just twenty-eight squadrons, twenty-one of which served in Empire areas overseas, with just seven for home defence.[6] Demobilization was carried out rapidly and thousands of aircraft were written off and destroyed, or sold to third parties abroad. The Aircraft Disposal Company, set up in 1919, handled 10,000 aircraft and 30,000 aero-engines.[7] RAF personnel at the end of the war numbered 30,122 officers and 253,410 other ranks. They had signed on for four years but no longer. Men could return to the navy or army if they wished, but there was now no guarantee of a post as the entire military apparatus contracted to peacetime levels. Financial stringency was imposed at once to try to limit the financial fall-out from four years of the costliest war in history. Thousands of officers assigned from the former RNAS abandoned the air force, either to return to the navy or to civilian life.[8] The remaining RAF officer corps was drawn heavily from men who had served in the RFC before April 1918, but most found themselves demobilized. By the autumn of 1919 the RAF had already shrunk to just 35,000 men, one tenth of its size at the conclusion of the war, with 1,500 officers, three quarters of them on short-term commissions for two to five years. The element working with the fleet, much to the dismay of the Admiralty, was reduced to just 140 officers and 4,000 other ranks.[9] The Air Council had hoped to retain the WRAF with a peacetime strength of 6,000 – the women's branch, the Council president suggested, 'would accord with the spirit of the times' – but Parliament rejected the idea. By March 1920, when the WRAF was wound up, there were just 376 women left in the force.[10] The small scale of the surviving air service in 1919 served to emphasize the temporary status of the wartime RAF and encouraged those military and naval predators who hoped to devour the air service for their own purposes.

The case for keeping the RAF as a permanent peacetime service was thrown again into jeopardy by a renewed crisis surrounding its leadership. Trenchard gave up command of the Independent Force on the day of the Armistice and handed his units back to John Salmond, commander of the RAF in France attached to the British Expeditionary Force. Trenchard's future in the RAF was entirely uncertain, and he doubted that any senior role would be granted him with Sykes as chief-of-staff. A few weeks later Lord Weir also announced his resignation. He told Lloyd George that he did not want in peacetime 'the collective and political responsibility of the whole Ministry'. He returned to his business interests and never held political office again, although he remained through to the 1930s an important adviser to governments on air force matters.[11] Weir's resignation was made on the day of the General Election called by Lloyd George at the end of the war, which was won overwhelmingly by his Liberal–Conservative coalition. The return to postwar conditions might have made it possible for Lloyd George to terminate the Air Ministry as a wartime improvisation, as other wartime ministries were wound up in the year following the Armistice. Instead he offered the post to Winston Churchill in tandem with the War Office, as Secretary of State for War and Air. This was not Churchill's first choice. At the end of the war he told Lloyd George that he contemplated leaving the Coalition government unless he was offered a 'key post' in the reconstructed Cabinet after the election.[12] Lloyd George preferred to have Churchill in the government rather than outside, and in late December offered him the choice of the War Office or the Admiralty, the post he had held at the start of the war. 'You can take the Air with you in either case,' Lloyd George is quoted as saying; 'I am not going to keep it as a separate department.'[13] Churchill replied that the choice was easy –'my heart is in the Admiralty' – but he suggested that the Air Ministry and air force would best be attached to the Admiralty and Royal Navy instead of remaining independent. Aircraft, Churchill wrote, 'will never be a substitute for armies', but they would become an 'economical substitute' for ships, an argument that would hardly have been welcomed by the navy's high command.[14] In the end, Lloyd George insisted on Churchill at the War Office with the Air Ministry added in. On 10 January Churchill accepted the joint appointment and took up his office four days later.[15]

If Lloyd George had hoped that fusing the army and air force under one ministerial appointment would eventually see the disappearance of the ministry and the RAF, Churchill became a sudden enthusiast for a separate air force. On 8 February he informed the Admiralty that 'the future independence of the Air Force and Air Ministry will in no way be prejudiced' by his appointment.[16] It is not clear why Churchill changed his mind, and later in the year he had second thoughts about whether it would not be more economical to divide the air forces between the army and navy, until he finally came out in full support of the idea that the air force might at some point 'obtain the primary place in the general conception of war policy' and ought to remain independent.[17] It seems unlikely that Churchill decided to support the air force in the prospect of enhancing his political reputation, since the Air Ministry was still a temporary institution with a low public profile. More probable is the role played by his almost boyish enthusiasm for flying, first expressed before the war when he flew with naval aviators 'for sheer joy and pleasure' and renewed in 1919 when he hoped to get a pilot's licence. His flying ended only after a crash on 18 July during a training flight at Croydon aerodrome, which left him severely bruised and his instructor with a broken leg. He was persuaded that flying was too dangerous an occupation for a senior minister of the Crown.[18]

1. RFC carpenters' repair shop

2. Frederick Sykes and the RFC administrative staff, 1912

3. Observer with camera, 16th Wing Photographic Section

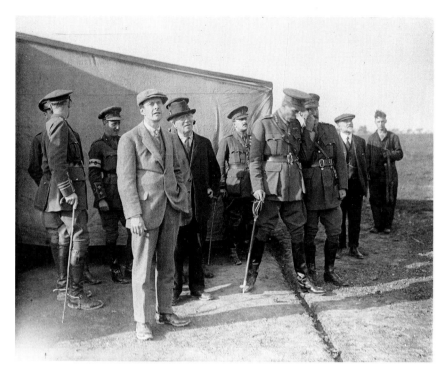

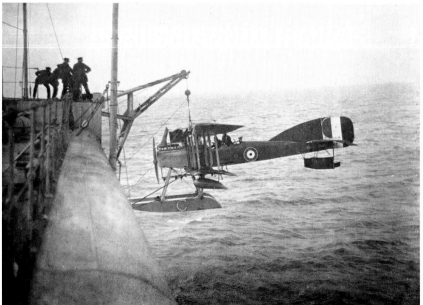

4. Hugh Trenchard and Herbert Asquith at the Western Front, 1916
5. Hoisting an RNAS seaplane on board

6. Temporary accommodation on the Strand outside Hotel Cecil
7. Aerial view of bombing of London, 7 July 1917

8.  Jan Smuts and Arthur Balfour, July 1917

9. RFC cadets at dinner in Christ Church, Oxford, October 1917

10. King George V and John Salmond at RFC HQ

11. Funeral of von Richthofen, the 'Red Baron', April 1918

12. RAF mechanics preparing targets for gunnery practice

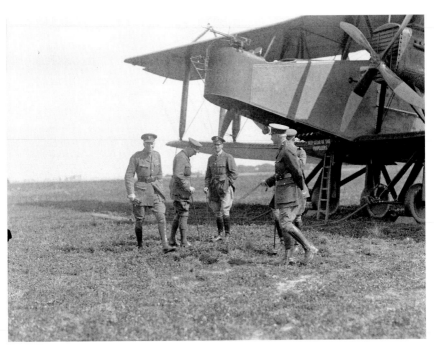

13. Handley Page O/400 heavy bomber, 1918

14. Training US officers in aerial gunnery

15. Cranwell at the end of its construction, 1922
16. Churchill and Trenchard at the Hendon Air Show, 1920

17. RAF Sopwith Snipes in Germany, March 1919

18. Siskin aircraft lined up at Hendon Air Show, 1929

19. Fleet Air Arm Fairey Swordfish torpedo bombers above the Solent

In the first week of February 1919 Churchill invited Trenchard to attend a meeting. Weir had advised reinstating the former chief-of-staff, despite the effective collaboration he had had with Sykes. Churchill wrote later that he had been happy to have Trenchard back, partly because he sympathized with his reasons for leaving his post in 1918, partly because in his view Trenchard had 'outstanding qualities' as a leader.[19] Trenchard was astonished to be offered the role he had resigned from almost a year before. He protested that Sykes was already in office, but Churchill told him that he had already decided to divide the military and civilian sectors and that Sykes was to be Director General of Civil Aviation. Trenchard then objected that he was unlikely to agree with Churchill's view of the RAF's future, but when he submitted a paper describing his policy for the RAF Churchill agreed to it, and Trenchard accepted the post. Why he did so is open to speculation. Trenchard's own recollection of the decision is brief and laconic: 'He said I must accept, and he pressed me to, so I agreed to come back as CAS.'[20] He did so, he told an RAF audience a few years later, 'with a good deal of alarm . . . I thought my effort likely to end in failure'.[21] Until that point, Trenchard's attitude to the new ministry and a separate air force had been almost entirely negative, even when he occupied the role of chief-of-staff briefly in early 1918. He found ministerial life uncongenial and was candid about his incapacities in the world of political and bureaucratic infighting. His view of the Independent Force he had commanded for five months was dismissive. The decision to accept the post must have owed something to Trenchard's own poor career prospects without a senior role, even though there was no certainty that a Chief of the Air Staff would still be in post later in 1919. He may have liked the fact that the War Office and the Air

Ministry were now under one portfolio, given his earlier preference for army aviation. The sidelining of Sykes also meant that Trenchard, as the most senior and experienced officer in the force, was free for the present to shape the air arm the way he wanted. Perhaps aware that his change of heart needed some justification both for himself and for others, he later wrote in notes for his biographer, in capital letters, 'I LEARNT AS I WENT ON'.[22] Whatever his motives, he was altered by his decision from an ambivalent observer of the young RAF to its foremost champion.

The force that Churchill and Trenchard now directed was in a state of turbulent dissolution. One of Churchill's first acts was to try to rescue a separate identity by insisting that the army ranks adopted by the RAF in April 1918 should be replaced by ranks that were particular to the air service. This Trenchard opposed without success, testament to his continued identity with the army he had served for more than twenty-five years. The adoption of army ranks in 1918 had simplified the transition to the RAF for the majority of the new force serving with the RFC. However, a tentative list had already been drawn up in 1917 employing a mix of army and navy ranks as well as ranks peculiar to the projected new air force – Air Marshal, Air Warden and Vice Warden, Commodore, Commander, Major, Captain, Lieutenant and Ensign – but it was not acted upon. Later in 1918, when the Air Ministry considered the size and distribution of a possible peacetime officer corps, the ranks were still the basic army categories from general down to lieutenant.[23] In early 1919, Churchill asked the Air Staff for their proposals for air force ranks, against the insistence by the Royal Navy that none of theirs should be appropriated and the army's preference for retaining the existing army nomenclature. The first attempt was little better than the suggestion of 'Air Warden' and 'Vice Warden' two years earlier: Air Marshal, Ardian, Squadron Ardian and Flight Ardian, titles loosely based, it was claimed, on the Gaelic words *ard* ('chief') and *eun* ('bird'). These were certainly more elegant than the suggestion that the equivalent rank to navy captain and army colonel should be 'Grouper'.[24] In the end, the agreed ranks reflected very closely the practice in the RNAS, with the exception of the senior ranks of Marshal of the Air, Air Chief Marshal, Air Marshal and Air Vice-Marshal. There was strong army opposition to the idea that 'air marshal' should mimic the title of 'field marshal' ('the ruination and degradation of a great name and a great rank' complained the Chief of the Imperial General Staff); the original request to the Crown to approve Marshal of the Air as the most senior rank was rejected by the King, who thought Marshal of the Air as pointless as 'Admiral of the Atlantic'.[25] The most senior rank was changed to Marshal of the Royal Air Force, though the King disliked this too and preferred the title 'Chief of the Air Force', which he used thereafter. The other ranks were modelled on the naval air service: Air Commodore, Group Captain, Wing Commander, Squadron Leader, Flight Lieutenant, Flying Officer, Pilot Officer. By Air Ministry Order 973 on 1 August 1919 the new ranks were confirmed as permanent, and have survived ever since.

The new ranks were applied to a rapidly shrinking body of officers, men and women. The Ministry plan in 1918 envisaged a small elite force of no more than 2,000 officers, with four generals, six colonels, twenty-five lieutenant-colonels, and so on. With the coming of peace, the officers all on temporary commissions were invited to apply for permanent status. Some 6,500 applied, but the Cabinet approved only 1,500 and the Ministry finally selected 1,005 on grounds that were inevitably arbitrary. Some officers were selected without difficulty, based on their wartime record. The future Commander-in-Chief of Bomber Command, Arthur Harris, was confirmed as a Major (soon changed to Squadron Leader) in the RAF on permanent commission early in 1919, against his expectations.[26] Yet it was also possible for a senior officer, with a fine war record, to struggle for permanent status. Acting Brigadier-General Percy Groves was chief-of-staff in the RFC Middle East Command and then, after the formation of the RAF, Director of Flying Operations in the Air Ministry. In September 1918 he applied for a permanent commission according to the instructions issued to the temporary officers in the RAF, which he assumed would be something of a formality. He was told only in May 1919, with his status uncertain, that he still had only a temporary commission, by which time he was representing the air force at the Versailles Conference. He was then informed that his rank as acting Brigadier-General was to be downgraded to Group Captain RAF, consistent with his formal army rank of Colonel, but Groves strongly objected to the change on the ground that the Europeans he negotiated with would not regard him seriously if he was a Captain rather than a General. He was granted a permanent commission only in March 1920, on condition he that he give up his commission in the army. In 1922 a frustrated Groves resigned his new rank as Group Captain, became a prolific author on air matters, and continued to call himself Brigadier-General. His correspondence from the early 1920s shows that he was not the only officer alienated by the change in rank title and the slow and unfathomable process in deciding who would and who would not hold a permanent commission.[27]

The Air Ministry was anxious, despite the problems surrounding demobilization and rank change, to establish a system of entry into the peacetime RAF that would bring in a fresh generation of young airmen who had not experienced the transition from one service to another. A committee on the 'Preliminary Education of Candidates for Royal Air Force Commissions' was set up under the air force officer and MP Hugh Cecil. Its report was submitted in March 1919. The first requirement was that every officer candidate should be physically capable of flying, even those destined for the scientific or administrative branches. Beyond that, the Committee focused on qualities of mind and temperament. 'A certain amount of intelligence is indispensable,' ran the report, but also 'a certain moral temper', summed up, it was suggested, by that ineffable English term 'a gentleman'. If possible, the successful officer candidate should have 'a high standard of courage, self-control, and honourable conduct, and seemly and considerate manners and deportment'. While not excluding men of 'small means and humble origins', the report recommended selecting from the universities and the public schools, including those 'who have a literary taste' as well as those with a scientific background.[28] The reputation of the later RAF for promoting men from public-school backgrounds, although less deserved as the air force became more technically advanced, was rooted in the initial preference for gentlemanly qualities. In November 1919, a cadet college was opened at Cranwell in Lincolnshire, where these qualities could be fully tested. The bias in favour of boys from public schools even extended to the first RAF Apprentice Scheme, established in 1920 to train a new generation of workers for the aero-engine, airframe and wireless trades. A dedicated educational programme for other ranks was in itself an innovation, and the most successful apprentices could move on to become commissioned officers themselves. Six years later, Trenchard told a gathering of RAF officers that his purpose was to recruit 'the intelligent class, who can learn quickly and absorb quickly'. Standards of entry remained high for the RAF through to the Second World War.[29]

The changes in personnel took place in a context where the very existence of the new service as a permanent feature of the defence establishment was called into question. Since commissions were at first still temporary, the whole organization suffered from a sense of impermanence. Survival through the early months of 1919 depended largely on inertia. The government faced a wide range of domestic problems, crisis across many areas of the Empire, and the large task of contributing to the peace settlement in Europe and the Middle East. The army and navy were faced with their own problems of large-scale demobilization, which postponed any renewed attempt to reabsorb air forces under their control. Churchill was heavily occupied with his responsibilities at the War Office and left his other portfolio largely in peace. The Air Ministry and Trenchard's staff took advantage of this moment of immunity to solidify the institutional structure of the air force, which had now moved out of the Hotel Cecil into permanent premises in nearby Kingsway, appropriately christened Adastral House. One of the first tasks was to establish all the ancillary branches that had been borrowed from the other services. These included medical and sanitary welfare, meteorological units, rationing, billeting and clothing. At the same time the ministry drew up the formal conditions for permanent commissions, rates of pay and pensions. This mundane work ensured that dismantling the whole operation would become an increasingly costly and legally complex task. The exact status of the RAF had nevertheless not yet been fully established. It existed in peculiar limbo, neither elevated to a secure future, nor yet dismantled as a redundant relic of the recent conflict.

In August 1919, Trenchard and his staff set out to establish the RAF on a more formal and permanent footing. In a memorandum on the 'Status of the Royal Air Force', prepared for a committee on national expenditure chaired by Eric Geddes, the chief-of-staff raised the central questions that had dominated the debate on a separate air force since 1917: should the RAF be capable of conducting its own independent operations under air force command? Or should it simply provide air force contingents 'as ancillary services' to the army and navy, under army and navy command? Trenchard now argued that the air force needed to be independent because multiple control by all three armed services 'reduced efficiency', the very argument he had used two years before against the idea of a new air service. The Air Ministry, he concluded, should have the right to allocate aircraft to the navy and army and to its own independent long-distance operations, a condition essential to an independent RAF.[30] The issue of permanence assumed a greater urgency when, in September, Churchill wavered briefly over the question of whether the cost of an air force was justified after the government had decided that defence expenditure should be cut back, based on the assumption that there would be no major war for at least ten years – soon to be popularly dubbed the 'Ten-Year Rule'. When Trenchard learned of Churchill's possible change of heart, he stormed into Churchill's office and engaged in a shouting match with his minister over the future of the force.[31] Later the same day, 11 September 1919, he drafted a second document that addressed the problem of the temporary character of a force set up in conditions of war 'owing to the great popular outcry' in 1917 about the state of the air services. This time he argued that a separate air force was essential to 'encourage and develop airmanship, or, better still, the Air spirit, like the Naval spirit, and to make it a force that will profoundly influence the strategy of the future'. The air force, he continued, had not had the luxury that the army and navy had had to develop over centuries, but had condensed 100 years of development into five short years, giving it a status that matched the other services. He concluded with a rhetorical question that once again sat oddly with his earlier arguments against change: 'how can you really progress in the Air except by a separate Air Force . . . ?'[32]

Churchill did not in the end renege on his initial commitment to maintain an independent ministry and air force. In late November the Air Staff drew up a third memorandum on the reconstruction of a permanent RAF, which they sent to Churchill for his approval. 'I agree,' he scribbled hurriedly on the draft.[33] Trenchard then produced a final document outlining the achievements so far in founding the force, the problems still to be overcome ('not one single permanent barracks', no government-owned stations except Cranwell), and the speculation that the role of an independent air force might become 'more and more the predominating factor in all types of warfare'.[34] This document was reproduced on 11 December 1919 for the Cabinet, prefaced with a covering note by Churchill, under the portentous title 'Royal Air Force: Permanent Organisation of the Royal Air Force'.[35] No political objections were raised, and the RAF at last achieved permanent status.

It turned out to be a fragile victory. Real independence for the air force proved to be a red rag to the bulls in the army and navy. What ought to have been the conclusion to an unstable period of construction was transformed by service rivalry into the starting point for years of fractious efforts to undo what Trenchard and his staff had achieved by the end of 1919. The ensuing conflict with both the navy and the army over the survival of an independent RAF was anticipated by Trenchard as he drew up the new terms of permanence. In November 1919 he informed the First Sea Lord, David Beatty, about the contents of his memorandum, promising that a portion of the air force would serve with the navy, a portion with the army, but the main portion would comprise an independent central core, likely to become the largest part. 'What is wanted in the Air Service,' he concluded, 'is a period of freedom from criticism by Parliament and the public' and the endless discussion by 'the large number of Naval and Army officers . . . who consider that the Air Force should be broken up'. At a face-to-face meeting with Beatty and the army Chief of the Imperial General Staff, Henry Wilson, Trenchard was able to extract a grudging year-long truce, but no promise that either service would abandon their intention to dismantle the RAF if they could.

The truce lasted a full year before the latent conflict resurfaced, but the sentiment of distrust and hostility did not disappear. Wilson noted in his diary in May 1920 after Churchill had agreed to allow the RAF to take a leading position in the pacification campaign in the League Mandate of Iraq, 'The sooner the Air Force crashes the better . . . It is a wicked waste of money as run at present'.[36] When in February 1921 Churchill, now Colonial Secretary rather than Secretary of State for War and Air, proposed to extend RAF responsibility throughout the Middle East, the army and navy joined forces to try once again to eliminate an independent RAF. The army General Staff prepared a memorandum for the new Secretary of War, Laming Worthington-Evans, setting out in detail their objections to the continued existence of the RAF: 'Aircraft at present and for many years to come must act as an auxiliary arm to the Naval and Military Services and as such should be organized, trained and employed as integral parts of these Services.' The army pointed out that no other country had adopted the British pattern, citing a comment from Franklin D. Roosevelt, former Assistant Secretary for the Navy in Washington, that the RAF was considered internationally as a 'costly failure'.[37] In forwarding the memorandum to the Committee of Imperial Defence, Worthington-Evans added that Marshal Foch, architect of victory in 1918, held strongly to the view that 'the principle of the absolute independence of the Air Service is inadmissable'. Neither the Committee of Imperial Defence nor the Cabinet were impressed by the arguments, but in September Wilson returned to the fray when Geddes was once again investigating possible cuts in national expenditure: 'we deprecate the divorcement of the Royal Air Force from the Army and Navy . . . we want as much Air Force and as little Air Ministry as we can get for our money'.[38] Trenchard for his part deplored this 'still more intemperate attack' and added 'the imagination of the soldier has evidently severe limitations', an accusation that might at one time have been directed at him. In preparing papers for Geddes' Committee, the Air Staff condemned the older services for seeing no further 'than their own limited horizons'.[39] Geddes' final report in December vindicated the RAF as good value for money but, ironically enough, cut the money available for navy and army cooperation.[40]

In 1922 the campaign against the RAF was renewed, but this time the chief antagonist was the Royal Navy. The Admiralty had since early 1919 always insisted that the navy respected the principle of a separate air service. But this principle did not exclude the strong desire to win back complete control over that portion assigned to work with the navy, particularly those units working directly with the main fleet. In March 1922

Beatty complained to Churchill that the navy disliked a situation in which their air equipment and personnel was supplied by another service 'over which we have no control'. A few months later he reiterated to Churchill the Admiralty view that a naval unit of the fighting fleet 'must be manned, administered and controlled by the Navy'.[41] Trenchard rejected what he saw as the navy's dissimulating claim: 'The Admiralty, and you can camouflage it how you will, are asking for a separate Air Service'. The Air Staff remained utterly opposed to what they saw as an attempt to turn the clock back to the situation in 1914.[42] The intransigence of the two services over the future of air power at sea was finally resolved by Lloyd George's successor as prime minister, Andrew Bonar Law, when a committee was set up under Lord Salisbury to investigate the taut relations between the three armed services. In July 1923, the committee found in favour of the RAF on the dispute between the air force and the navy over personnel and equipment. For the time being, the Air Ministry kept overall control over naval aviation and a unitary RAF.[43] The following year Trenchard and Vice-Admiral Roger Keyes negotiated a final agreement that gave the Admiralty operational authority over what was called the Fleet Air Arm, a branch of the RAF on permanent secondment to naval vessels at sea. The Fleet Air Arm was formally constituted on 1 April 1924.[44]

There are a number of ways in which the repeated efforts of the naval and military high commands to break up the RAF might be explained. The most straightforward is simply a question of service jealousy. In the current climate of close collaboration between the three armed services, it is difficult to understand why in the early twentieth century the services saw each other as competitors rather than colleagues, each guarding its own role and identity, each scrambling for a share of the limited defence budget. In this case, however, rivalry was based on more fundamental issues. The two areas in which the RAF assumed a leading role after the war, in home defence and imperial policing, were both the traditional responsibility of the older services. The idea that British imperial territory and the British homeland could better be protected or policed by aircraft was a radical departure, certain to arouse resentment and argument over the merits of the upstart service.

The role of aircraft in imperial security was an unpredictable outcome of the rapid wartime development of British air power, summed up in Sykes' memorandum at the end of the war on the future of the RAF when he suggested that the 'Air Force must be the first line of defence of the British Empire'.[45] The first use of aircraft for the defence of empire was modest enough. In May 1919, aircraft were used in the Third Afghan War in raids against the cities of Dakka and Jalalabad. One raid was made on the Afghan capital of Kabul by the only operational Handley Page V/1500 heavy bomber, the aircraft originally intended for a bombing offensive against Germany in 1919. Though the damage was slight, the raid encouraged the Afghan leaders to abandon the war. However, the campaign that provoked the first fears of the older services about RAF ambitions was conducted against the so-called 'Mad Mullah', the Somali religious leader Mohammed Abdulla Hassan, and his Dervish supporters. Two squadrons of just eight aircraft were sent to British Somaliland and began a five-day bombing campaign in January 1920 before army units moved in. The pacification was a limited success at best, but there followed an argument between the air force and the army over who might claim it. For Trenchard and the fledgling service, the air control of the empire opened up important possibilities, not only justifying an independent air force, but also demonstrating that air power was a much cheaper way of policing Britain's global territories than army expeditionary forces and naval intervention.

Over the following two years, with Churchill's strong support at the Colonial Office, the RAF developed a scheme for the policing of the Middle East, where Britain now had additional territorial responsibilities in Palestine, Transjordan and Mesopotamia (modern-day Iraq) following the granting of mandates from the League of Nations. Iraq was the most important of the three because of widespread resistance to British control, but here was a case where army responsibility had been clear. The decision of the Cabinet to approve the air policing of the territory, under an RAF Supreme Commander, challenged military prerogatives, and occasioned the long campaign in 1921 and 1922 to break up the air force. Air control in Iraq began on 1 October 1922 under the command of the former Commander-in-Chief of the RAF in France, John Salmond, who used aircraft ruthlessly not only against insurgents but also at times to enforce the payment of taxes.[46] The army chafed at the bit over the limitations imposed on its own operations, but the Air Ministry argument that air policing saved the taxpayer substantial sums was vindicated when a committee under Lord Colwyn, established in August 1925 to investigate RAF expenditure, confirmed the air force claim.[47] To demonstrate the apparent effectiveness of the RAF's new imperial role, the annual RAF tournament at Hendon aerodrome in north London climaxed with a flight of aircraft dropping small incendiary bombs on a model of an African village.

Service jealousy, though real enough, was not an argument. Both the older services found solid reasons to question the real effectiveness of aircraft acting independently. Postwar investigation of the long-range bombing campaign provided no evidence that the raids had made any difference to the outcome of the war, while the navy insisted that bombing civilian areas was contrary to international law. In 1921, the army General Staff dismissed the idea that bombing could possibly be decisive, though in terms that must have worried the politicians who read it: 'London might be laid in ruins, the House of Commons, the Admiralty and the War Office might have to function in disused coalmines or other subterranean refuges, the national life might be dislocated to an unprecedented degree, but that would not of itself force a decision . . .'[48] Air defence was also rejected by the army General Staff as a justification for a separate air force. The original aim in 1917 to establish an air force to defend Britain, and London in particular, against air attack was shown by the official statistics to have been in their view largely a failure.

For their part, the Royal Navy deprecated the loss of their principal role in defending the home islands from possible attack. In January 1919 the navy informed the War Cabinet that the response to the threat of invasion of the home islands was their responsibility, and consequently that it made sense to give them control of coastal aircraft to work with the fleet in repelling enemy air and sea operations. Air attacks on inland centres, the Admiralty gracelessly conceded, 'would appear to be the responsibility of the Air Ministry'.[49] The navy argument that any enemy crossing the sea ought sensibly to be engaged first by the fleet and by supporting aircraft under naval command rumbled on for some years thereafter. There were good grounds for doubting the capacity of the RAF to deliver effective Empire defence. At one point early in 1920 there were only two fully serviceable RAF squadrons available for home defence, a puny force to meet any possible air attack on the United Kingdom, unlikely though it might have been. In India the RAF was starved of aircraft, spares and mechanics, and the small handful of aircraft available were for the most part not serviceable. In Ireland, the limited number of aircraft allocated for the 'Defence of Ireland Scheme' were poorly maintained; at one station in the west of the island there was for a time only a single serviceable aircraft. The men lived mostly in tents in conditions described after one investigation as 'squalid to the last degree'.[50] Under these circumstances, the argument that the air force ought to supersede the other services in defence of the homeland and Empire seemed at best unconvincing.

The Air Staff and their combative chief did not take the arguments of the other services lying down. In response to naval claims that the Senior Service should be responsible for defending the home islands, the Air Staff counterattacked by circulating a memorandum on the 'Big Ship Controversy' that foresaw the disappearance of the old-fashioned capital ship once enough resources had been devoted to the air. 'In the past,' the document continued, 'one of the roles of our Navy has been to protect these islands from invasion: the Air Staff has no hesitation in saying that the Air Force of the present . . . is an adequate counter to this menace.'[51] The Fleet Air Arm, claimed a later memorandum, is an integral part of the RAF, not 'part of the Navy'. Trenchard told Churchill in March 1922, at the height of the naval controversy, that he started from the basis, 'from which we cannot depart, that the Air Service is one complete whole', not one to be divided up to suit the other services.[52] Nevertheless, the RAF position remained vulnerable. Most of the assertions about air power lay in the future, as the army and navy both realized. In autumn 1922 the Lloyd George coalition collapsed and a Conservative administration under Andrew Bonar Law took its place. By fateful coincidence, Sykes had married Bonar Law's eldest daughter. When his father-in-law asked for advice on the future of the Air Ministry, Sykes mischievously suggested that the RAF should be broken up and returned to the other services. The new Air Minister, Samuel Hoare, was told that he might not occupy his new portfolio for very long. In late October that year Trenchard wrote to one of his senior commanders about the latest crisis: 'frankly I think (though I may be wrong) that I may not be much longer in office'.[53]

Why did the RAF maintain an independent existence in the face of so much pressure to return to the pre-war defence establishment? The simple answer is that the RAF was saved by the politicians, a conclusion that Trenchard, with his inveterate distrust of the world of politics, would have been reluctant to endorse. Trenchard himself proved to be a more adroit political operator than his diffidence about office work or his reputation for blunt talk, serial resignation and muddled thinking might have suggested. Yet time and again when it seemed the future of the RAF was seriously in doubt, senior political players were willing to campaign on its behalf. In 1919 the key figure was Churchill, despite his occasional doubts. It was Churchill who defended in Cabinet the change to permanent status for the RAF in December 1919; it was Churchill at the Colonial Office who insisted in 1921 that the RAF draw up a plan for air policing in the Middle East. Churchill told Trenchard, according to a later account, that it was his chance 'to establish the Air Force as a separate service beyond doubt'.[54] In the renewed crisis over the future of the force in 1922, it was Churchill who wrote to the Foreign Secretary, Austen Chamberlain, in March that year explaining that the uncertainty surrounding the future status of the RAF was damaging the service and asking him to state categorically in a Commons debate that there was no intention of winding it up. Chamberlain obliged with a parliamentary statement on 16 March that made the present government's position clear: 'Believing, however, as we do that the Air Forces have immense potentialities of their own, and in their own element . . . we consider that it would be a retrograde step at this time to abolish the Air Ministry and to reabsorb the Air Service into the Admiralty and the War Office.'[55]

The advent of the Bonar Law government in August 1922 led to a brief renewal of the argument about a separate air force, but the new Secretary of State for Air, Samuel Hoare, became an instant supporter of an independent service. He held the office, except for a brief interlude in 1924, for seven years, the longest-serving air minister, and with his unstinting support the RAF survived the investigation into service co-operation instigated by Bonar Law in March 1923. The Sub-Committee of the Committee of Imperial Defence under Lord Salisbury, the Lord President of the Council, reported in July that year, confirming once again the political preference for an independent RAF. Inter-service collaboration, which had been one of the objects of investigation, was to be maintained by the recently established Chiefs-of-Staff Committee, an initiative that Trenchard had helped to set up deliberately in order to ensure that the RAF would sit on an equal basis with the navy and army to decide Britain's defence strategy.[56] Hoare's Principal Private Secretary, Christopher Bullock, recalled that 'ministers found the Air Ministry case unanswerable.' Trenchard admitted years afterwards that the survival of the RAF 'owed a lot to the Salisbury Committee'.[57] This was not yet the end of the story. The Admiralty refused to accept the terms of the Salisbury report, and Hoare battled on the RAF's behalf to prevent any further attempt to subvert the clear decision that the naval air forces were part of the RAF. Finally in 1926, Stanley Baldwin, the Conservative prime minister, lost patience with naval intransigence. He told the House of Commons that the organization of imperial defence was now based on 'three co-equal services', sharing responsibility for British security: 'controversy upon this subject must now cease.'[58] After eight years of what the RAF Director of Intelligence described as 'a very gruelling business' – fighting the army, the navy and the Treasury – the RAF no longer faced an uncertain future.[59]

Political support for the RAF continued the tradition established in 1917 when Lloyd George overrode military objections to force through the inauguration of the new service. The British constitutional system required that a reform of this magnitude should be the responsibility of Parliament, but it also meant that the older services had no real power to affect the politicians' decision. Churchill reminded Austen Chamberlain in March 1922 that the RAF was created by Act of Parliament and the statute could only be undone by a parliamentary decision to repeal it, not by what Churchill called 'mischievous inter-departmental agitation'. In Parliament there existed a strident lobby on behalf of British air power which would, in Churchill's words, 'oppose and obstruct to the utmost any measure of repeal'.[60] Moreover, the formal creation of the RAF had been the responsibility of the monarch, George V, who now bore the title 'Chief of the Air Force' and who was not likely, given the support he had already displayed for the RAF, to relinquish the title lightly.

The King was a regular guest at the Hendon Tournament (later the 'air pageant'), an event that grew in popularity with the spread of what was called 'airmindedness'. The first tournament in 1920 attracted more than 40,000 people, with additional crowds gathered outside the airfield to watch the displays of mock combat and aerobatics. Aviation was big news in the 1920s, whether long-distance endurance flights, or exploration of the little known areas of the globe, or air circuses and displays. The Air Ministry was also responsible for organizing the development of British civil aviation in the 1920s. The novelty of regular commercial flight for those who could afford it helped to shape an increasingly sympathetic public opinion after the critical attitude toward British air performance during the war. It also meant that the future of Britain in the air was a civilian as well as a military issue.

The popular interest in aviation was reflected in the willingness of the politicians to exploit the air as a novel solution to difficult issues of imperial security. Even before the end of the war, the British Viceroy in Ireland, trying to cope with the threat of a national uprising, was calling on the RAF to use bombs and machine-guns to 'put the fear of God into these playful young Sinn Feiners'.[61] Though the 'Defence of Ireland Scheme' drawn up by the RAF in 1919 was difficult to operate with any success, the politicians saw the air force as an instrument capable of overcoming the limitations of the army presence. The RAF was sent to Russia as a contribution to the anti-Bolshevik campaign waged in 1918–19 by the Allied powers. The development of air policing of the Empire was welcomed by the government not only as a way to cut costs, which was a prime consideration, but because the exercise of air power was shown to work. Henry Dobbs, the British High Commissioner in Iraq, and an early sceptic about the value of an RAF campaign, concluded in 1924 that air control had been 'brilliantly, magnificently successful'.[62] The financial argument for governments that were committed to defence retrenchment in the 1920s was unassailable. The cost of the military occupation of Iraq in 1920–21 had been £32 million, in 1921–2 it was £23 million; in the year following the assumption of RAF command in the region, the cost was £6.6 million and by 1927–8 that sum had been reduced to just £1.65 million.[63] The fiscal implications helped to underwrite the growing awareness that air power was a cost-effective way of maintaining empire security. 'I think the Air Force,' Churchill later claimed, 'was a great economy in maintaining order in these wild countries.'[64]

Finally, the political appeal of the RAF was bound up with public and government anxiety in the early 1920s that the rapid demobilization of the air force left Britain vulnerable to any possible attack from the air. The fear of the 'knock-out blow', as it came to be known, was evidently exaggerated, since no neighbouring air force in the early 1920s was capable of delivering such a blow even if it were feasible, while the evidence from the bombing during the war showed that the effects of bomb attack were much more limited than the postwar fantasies suggested.[65] The fear, nevertheless, was real enough. In 1922 the Committee of Imperial Defence discussed the possibility that an enemy air force could drop 300 tons within 48 hours, and 100 tons per day for a month thereafter. There was talk of putting the population under martial law if this happened, with absentee workers treated as 'deserters'.[66] The prospective 'enemy' in this case was France. A year before, the Committee had been presented with tabulated statistics showing the air strength of the major powers. French air forces now dwarfed the RAF, and, even if a sudden French air strike seemed implausible, British leaders considered the possibility that the French government might use the threat of a bombing campaign to make Britain a more pliant onlooker as France came to dominate the European continent. Arthur Balfour thought that in the face of the French menace Britain was 'more defenceless than it has ever been before'. [67] That year the Defence Committee established yet another sub-committee on the 'Continental Air Menace', the product of a similar paranoia that had fuelled the naval race against Germany before 1914. The French 'Air Division' set up to perform strategic tasks was known to possess almost 600 fighters and bombers. Intelligence assessments added the thirty-four other French squadrons and French civil aircraft to paint a gloomy picture of Britain's helpless plight in the air. The menace, fanciful though it proved to be, helped to change Bonar Law's mind about the RAF. Having flirted with breaking the air force up, he came to see its expansion as a pressing response to the temporary imbalance of air power against Britain's erstwhile wartime ally. One of the recommendations of the Salisbury Committee when it reported in July 1923 was to endorse a planned RAF home defence strength of 600 aircraft to match the French 'Air Division'.[68]

There seems little doubt that Trenchard and the Air Staff played up the idea of Britain's vulnerable position in the air against France to win political support for a larger air force organized independently of the other services. The result was a political victory for the RAF in its struggle for recognition. In mid-1922, Trenchard drafted a revised scheme for home defence to meet the current alleged danger. In place of the three squadrons currently available to defend the British Isles, he recommended a force of twenty-three squadrons. Consistent with the view he and other senior airmen had held during the war that the best defence was offence, the force was divided between fighters intended to defend against incoming bombers, and day and night bombing squadrons to inflict a counter-blow against the enemy.[69] In August that year the Cabinet accepted what came to be called the Home Defence Air Force. The RAF argument that only a strong air force could counter the strategic vulnerability of the country was accepted by the politicians, and on 9 July 1923 the force was formally approved by the government with wide public support, giving the RAF a rationale that neither the army nor navy could challenge. The Home Defence Air Force proved difficult to establish quickly, given the financial constraints and the failure under Trenchard's leadership to move fast enough out of the biplane age. In 1925 the government postponed completion of the force until 1935 under the 'Ten-Year Rule', by which time the French 'menace' had evaporated and the force seemed less urgent. Nevertheless, the policy decisions in 1922–3 ensured that the RAF would be regarded by the politicians as the primary means of defending the heart of the Empire.[70]

One central question ran through all the arguments and counter-arguments in the years after the end of the war: what was the RAF for? In the last months of the war this question was never fully answered, since most aircraft continued to give direct support to the army and navy, despite the expectation that home defence and strategic bombing would really give the RAF a claim to full service independence. In April 1919, a convalescent Trenchard wrote to Churchill with brief thoughts about the postwar air force. The most pressing need, Trenchard wrote, was to define 'for what purpose we are and with what object is the RAF being maintained'.[71] This proved to be a difficult proposition. RAF doctrine, to the extent that it was understood at the time, remained unclear, contradictory and speculative for much of the inter-war period. The main difficulty, a profound one for Trenchard as the great wartime champion of air support for the army, was to disengage the RAF from its principal wartime role as an auxiliary to the older services. The failure to do so would open up the objection that the air force was better off divided by function, part for the air-sea war, part to support the land war. This was how the air service was organized in all other major states where there was no separate air service. As the world's first independent air force the RAF faced the problem of creating a body of doctrine that justified that accolade. Whether airmen liked it or not, the situation pushed the RAF to argue for bombing and home defence as their strategic preference and to abandon as central aims the counter-force and ground support tactics deployed with great effect during the war, but both of which tied the air force too closely to the other services.

This doctrinal choice emerged only slowly, and with much uncertainty, in the early years of the new air force. When Trenchard set out the case for a permanent RAF in late 1919 he still suggested that a portion of the air force would be assigned to the army, a portion to the navy. A naval Fleet Air Arm did develop after much argument about who really controlled naval aviation, but the naval dimension of the RAF featured little if at all in Air Staff discussions about the nature of air strategy. By the time the Fleet Air Arm was finally assigned to Admiralty control in July 1937, British naval aviation was far behind those navies with a dedicated naval air force such as the United States and Japan. An army cooperation element remained largely on paper until the creation of what proved to be the painfully obsolescent Advanced Air Striking Force in autumn 1939, sent from Bomber Command to support the army in France after the declaration of a second world war, alongside a small number of fighter squadrons.

The German Air Force by contrast was almost entirely dedicated to supporting the ground offensive and destroying the enemy air force. Although support for surface forces and counter-force strategy did not disappear as an element of air doctrine, they were relegated to a back seat. The Manual of Combined Operations published later in the 1930s conceded only that 'the Army may need help . . .' in advancing against the enemy on land, not that air–ground collaboration was a vital dimension of modern war. Only three and a half pages out of 272 were devoted to air–army cooperation, one third of those to 'Control of Semi-Civilised Tribes within our own Jurisdiction'.[72] Until 1939, the prevailing hope in government was that a major land war in Europe could be avoided, which explains the low priority given to tactical air power. In March 1939 the Air Ministry finally drew up a specification for an aircraft that could do for the army exactly what they had done in the Great War ('close and distant tactical reconnaissance by day, observation of artillery fire, photography, low-level or shallow dive-bombing, and supply dropping'), but the slow two-seat design was obsolete even on paper, and never materialized.[73] When it became necessary to prepare for possible ground support against enemy troops, a mere seven pilots were trained in shallow dive-bombing, dropping just fifty-six bombs in practice. The Director of Plans at the Air Ministry, John Slessor, expressed a view common among airmen that 'the aeroplane is not a battlefield weapon'.[74] Before the Battle of France, when the AASF was also supposed to prepare for bombing operations against the enemy air force, RAF commanders continued to insist that this was an ineffective use of air resources, which ought to be directed at larger and more vulnerable industrial objectives in Germany itself. Unlike 1918, when Trenchard regarded the suppression of enemy air power as the first call on air resources, the RAF went to war in 1939 convinced that counter-force was no longer a viable strategic option. [75]

From the onset of imperial air policing, when light bombers were used to coerce recalcitrant tribesmen, long-range independent bombing came to be seen as the characteristic strategy for a modern air force. Once Trenchard was allowed to construct the Home Defence force, he openly campaigned along with his staff for a striking force to attack the enemy home front as the quickest and most effective way of compelling an enemy to give up. This remained a matter of faith, since there was no evidence to support the argument. Like Douhet in Italy, the British Air Staff simply assumed that, for modern urban populations, bombing on a large scale must be unendurable. In a speech to War Office staff in April 1923, Trenchard spelt out his vision of what air power ought to achieve:

> It is probable that any war on the European Continent in which we might be involved in the future would resolve itself, virtually, into a contest of morale between the respective civilian populations. By this is meant that there would be a tendency for the nationals of the power which suffered most from air attack, or which lacked in moral tenacity, to bring such pressure to bear on their government as to result in military capitulation.[76]

To army and navy objections that the true nature of strategy was to engage and overcome the enemy armed forces in combat, the air force countered that air power directed at an enemy's national centres 'is not to avoid fighting, but to win the war'. This meant choosing targets that would have 'the greatest effect on enemy will power' and would bring the war to an end in the shortest time.[77] These were assertions rather than strategic principles, but the idea that air power could shorten wars, or even win them single-handedly, had an appealing logic to a force determined to demonstrate its strategic independence. When the army and navy challenged the RAF in 1928 to define more precisely what was the 'War Aim of an Air Force', on the grounds that bombing in the Great War had been both ineffective and illegal, the Air Staff persisted with the idea that bombing the enemy's home front was the RAF's principal aim. Trenchard argued that air power afforded the opportunity to attack the enemy where he was weakest, rather than where he was strong. Enemy cities and industry were 'the points where defence is most difficult for him and where he is most vulnerable to attack by the air weapon'.[78] This speculation remained the central element of the RAF's approach to future war right down to 1940, when in May of that year the first long-distance raids against German cities began.

The emphasis on the offensive nature of air power meant that RAF commanders were much less interested in the issue of air defence at home, even though, to satisfy popular and political anxieties, the Home Defence Air Force was also designed to act as a shield against an enemy's air incursions.[79] Home defence could not be ignored, but the view that Trenchard had held in the war, that the best defence was a counter-offensive, remained another article of faith. When in the 1930s successive governments insisted that the RAF develop a major defensive capability, the Air Staff thought there was too much emphasis on defence. In a paper drafted in the summer of 1938, the staff returned to the question that Smuts had posed in his reports in 1917 about how to win a war. Defence did not win wars; instead, the paper continued, 'we must regard the Air Striking Force as constituting not only a strong deterrent and insurance in peace, but also as our only means of imposing our will on the enemy in war.'[80] This claim highlighted a strategic paradox that ran through all the interwar years: air defence was supposed to blunt any enemy bombing campaign, but an enemy would not in turn be able to prevent an RAF counter-offensive. In spring 1939 the Commander-in-Chief of Fighter Command, Air Chief Marshal Hugh Dowding, wrote to the Chief of Air Staff, Cyril Newall, claiming that any German bombing campaign against Britain 'would be brought to a standstill in a month or less' as a result of the casualties imposed by the air defenders.[81] At the same time the Air Ministry was preparing the so-called Western Air Plans, in which bombing German industrial centres played a central part, on the assumption that German air defences would not do the same as Fighter Command. Neither assumption proved correct, though Dowding was much closer to the truth, but the RAF retained well into the Second World War its paradoxical commitment to the view that offence and defence would be equally effective.

By this stage the RAF had been reorganized into functional categories that reflected the priority of an independent air strategy. In 1936, the force was split between Bomber Command, Fighter Command and Coastal Command. There was no dedicated tactical air force and no command for air–army cooperation. The legacy of the Great War, when counter-force and ground support had been paramount, had to be learned anew in the Second World War. When it was, British tactical air power arguably became the most important and successful development in the history of the RAF during its second major war. Bombing the home front, on the other hand, had not been well prepared and proved to be strategically dubious, lengthy rather than the swift knock-out blow, and costly to both friend and foe. British tactical air campaigns also demonstrated that institutional independence and service cooperation were not incompatible. When the war began, the one element in the RAF's new organization that was technically up to date and reasonably prepared was the fighter defence of the British Isles. By a peculiar irony the pressure of the politicians in the 1930s to find an effective defence against bombing brought the air force back full circle to the crisis in 1917 that had prompted the call for a separate service in the first place. The Battle of Britain was in this sense the fruit of a long gestation from the feeble defences of 1917–18 to the sophisticated air defence system of 1940.

Another twist of fate that year brought to power Winston Churchill, whose support for the fledgling RAF had played such an important part in the survival of an independent force. That support wavered at times again in the Second World War as it had in 1919, but in a speech in Boston, Massachusetts, thirty years after his brief spell as Air Minister, Churchill returned to the theme that air power was the future: 'For good or ill, air mastery is today the supreme expression of military power and Fleets and Armies, however necessary, must accept a subordinate rank.'[82] If Churchill's prognosis did not quite work out as he expected, the air service that he championed years before lit the flame for all the independent air forces that followed.

# NOTES

## 1. Britain and the War in the Air

1 H.G. Wells, *The War in the Air* (London: George Bell & Sons, 1908), p. 208.

2 H. G. Wells, *Experiment in Autobiography* (Boston: Little, Brown, 1934), p. 569.

3 Andrew Whitmarsh, 'British Army Manoeuvres and the Development of Military Aviation, 1910–1913', *War in History*, 14 (2007), pp. 326–7; Liddell Hart Archive Centre (LHA), Brooke-Popham papers, 8/3, 'A Brief History of the British Air Service, 1910–1935' (n.d.), pp. 1–2.

4 Frederick Sykes, *From Many Angles: An Autobiography* (London: Harrap, 1942), pp. 95–7. The motto is also used by the Australian, Canadian and New Zealand air forces, and was used by the Indian air force until 1947. The translation of *ardua* as 'adversity' is the preferred RAF version, but it can also mean 'struggle' or 'effort'.

5 Churchill College Archive Centre (CCAC), CHAR 13/6B/265, Churchill to Capt. Murray Sueter, 31 May 1914. Churchill wanted the title to be the Flying Wing.

6 The National Archive (TNA), AIR 1/727/149/1, Maj.-Gen. Sefton Brancker, 'Home Defence and Reorganisation of the RFC, 1914–1917' (n.d.), pp. 1–2.

7 Whitmarsh, 'British Army Manoeuvres', pp. 329–36; LHA, Brooke-Popham papers, 8/3, 'A brief history', p. 5.

8 LHA, Brooke-Popham papers, 1/8, RAF Staff College Notes, Dec 1924, 'Air Strength on the Western Front: Development and

Order of Battle'; 8/3, 'A Brief History', p. 5; TNA, AIR 1/718/29/8, Cmd. 100, 'Synopsis of British Air Effort during the War', Apr 1919, p. 16; Christopher Luck, 'The Smuts Report: Interpreting and Misinterpreting the Promise of Air Power', in Gary Sheffield and Peter Gray (eds.), *Changing War: The British Army, The Hundred Days Campaign and the Birth of the Royal Air Force, 1918* (London: Bloomsbury, 2013), pp. 150–51. RNAS figures are from Stephen Roskill (ed.), *Documents Relating to the Naval Air Service: Volume I, 1908–1918* (London: Navy Records Society, 1969), p. 747.

9  LHA, Brig.-Gen. Percy Groves papers, Box 2 (a), lecture by Groves on 'The Organisation and Work of the Royal Flying Corps', 3 Feb 1917, p. 3.

10  LHA, Brooke-Popham papers, 8/2, Training Manual, Royal Flying Corps, Part II (Military Wing), p. 82.

11  LHA, Brooke-Popham papers, RAF Field Service Book, Apr 1918, p. 74; 8/2, Training Manual, Royal Flying Corps, p. 28.

12  Royal Air Force Museum, Hendon (RAFM), B2717, transcript of diary kept by Air Mech. 2, Thomas Spencer, 66th Squadron RFC.

13  Paul Marr, 'Haig and Trenchard: Achieving Air Superiority on the Western Front', *Air Power Review*, 17 (2014), p. 32; John Slessor, *The Central Blue: Recollections and Reflections* (London: Cassell, 1956), p. 24. See too Trevor Nash, 'Flight Training in the First World War and its Legacy', *Air Power Review*, 19 (2016), pp. 38–41.

14  LHA, Brooke-Popham papers, 8/2, Training Manual, Royal Flying Corps, pp. 27–8.

15  LHA, Groves papers, 2 (a), 'The Organization and work of the Royal Flying Corps', 3 Feb 1917, p. 6.

16  Ibid., pp. 7–10.

17  LHA, Brooke-Popham papers, 8/2, Training Manual, Royal Flying Corps, Dec 1915.

18  CCAC, CHAR 13/29/194, draft statement by Churchill to House of Commons, 23 Nov 1914; R. D. Layman, *Naval Aviation in the First World War: Its Impact and Influence* (London: Chatham Publishing, 1996), pp. 37–8.

19  Roskill (ed.), *Naval Air Service: Volume I*, pp. 179, 309, 408–9; Layman, *Naval Aviation in the First World War*, pp. 74–5.

20  Maurice Baring, *Flying Corps Headquarters, 1914–1918* (London: Buchan & Enright, 1985), p.66.

21  Ibid., p. 64.

22  Basil Collier, *Heavenly Adventurer: Sefton Brancker and the Dawn of British Aviation* (London: Secker & Warburg, 1959), p. 46.

23  Russell Miller, *Trenchard: Father of the Royal Air Force* (London: Weidenfeld & Nicolson, 2016), pp. 100–102.

24  Sykes, *From Many Angles*, pp. 144–6.

25  Cambridge University Library (CUL), Boyle papers, Add 9429/1B/265, Trenchard to Major Lockhart (his first biographer), 3 Feb 1953.

26  RAFM, papers of MRAF Sir John Salmond, AC 71/20/B2644, 'C.F.S. Reminiscences', p. 2.

27  CUL, Boyle papers, Add 9429/1B/268 (i), 'Notes on a chapter written by Major Lockhart', 18 Jan 1954, p. 1.

28  Ibid., 1B/273 (i), Trenchard to Lockhart, 10 Oct 1958.

29  Eric Ash, *Sir Frederick Sykes and the Air Revolution 1912–1918* (London: Frank Cass, 1999), pp. 65–7.

30  Jerry White, *Zeppelin Nights: London in the First World War* (London: Bodley Head, 2014), pp. 125–6.

31  For the best recent account see Guillaume de Syon, *Zeppelin: Germany and the Airship, 1900–1939* (Baltimore, MD: Johns Hopkins University Press, 2002), pp.103–6.

32  Susan Grayzel, *At Home and Under Fire: Air Raid Culture in Britain from the Great War to the Blitz* (Cambridge: Cambridge University Press, 2012), pp. 25–31.

33  Layman, *Naval Aviation in the First World War*, p. 71.

34  TNA, AIR 9/5, note by the Chief of the Imperial General Staff on Mr Balfour's Memorandum, 16 Sep 1921.

35  TNA, AIR 1/718/29/8, Cmd. 100, 'Synopsis of the British Air Effort during the War', Apr 1919, p. 10.

36  TNA, AIR 1/721/46/4, Home Office, Home Defence Anti-Aircraft Precautions (Civilian), 1914–1918 (n.d.), pp. 3–4, 40–53.

37  LHA, Brooke-Popham papers, 8/3, 'A Brief History', p. 5.

38  J. M. Bruce, *The Aeroplanes of the Royal Flying Corps (Military Wing)* (London: Putnam, 1982), passim.

39  TNA, AIR 8/2, Brig.-Gen. David Henderson, 'Memorandum on the Organisation of the Air Service', 19 Jul 1917, pp. 2–3; AIR 9/5, 'Note by the Air Staff on the reasons for the formation of the Royal Air Force' (n.d., but 1921), pp. 1–2; Malcolm Cooper, 'Blueprint for Confusion: The Administrative Background to the Formation of the Royal Air Force, 1912–19', *Journal of Contemporary History*, 22 (1987), pp. 438–9; Peter Gray, 'The Air Ministry and the Formation of the Royal Air Force' in Sheffield, Gray (eds), *Changing War*, pp. 135–6.

40  TNA, AIR 8/2, 'First Report of the Air Board', 23 Oct 1916; Balfour for the Cabinet, 'A Reply to the First Report of the Air Board', 6 Nov 1916; Lord Curzon for the Cabinet, 'Last Words on the Air Board Controversy', 15 Nov 1916.

41  TNA, AIR 9/5, 'Note by the Air Staff on the reasons for the formation of the Royal Air Force' (1921), p. 3; AIR 8/2, Curzon, 'Last Words', p. 1. Curzon claimed that he had been given assurance not only that the Air Board's powers would be strengthened, but also that it would eventually be turned into an air ministry.

42  Gray, 'The Air Ministry', pp. 136–7; Cooper, 'Blueprint for Confusion', p. 439.

43  TNA, AIR 1/718/29/8, 'Synopsis of the British Air Effort', p. 16.

## 2. Battles in the Sky, Battles in Whitehall

1 TNA, AIR/1/718/29/9, memorandum by Hugh Cecil for Trenchard, 26 Aug 1917, p. 3.

2 TNA, WO 158/947, Intelligence Section, GHQ, Home Forces, 'Air Raids 1917', Jul 1917, pp. 3–4.

3 Jerry White, *Zeppelin Nights: London in the First World War* (London: Bodley Head, 2014), pp. 211–13.

4 Susan Grayzel, *At Home and Under Fire: Air Raids and Culture in Britain from the Great War to the Blitz* (Cambridge: Cambridge University Press, 2012), pp. 72–3; White, *Zeppelin Nights*, p. 214.

5 Christopher Luck, 'The Smuts Report: Interpreting and Misinterpreting the Promise of Air Power', in Gary Sheffield and Peter Gray (eds.), *Changing War: The British Army, the Hundred Days Campaign and the Birth of the Royal Air Force, 1918* (London: Bloomsbury, 2013), pp. 153–4.

6 Parliamentary Archives (P.Arch), Lloyd George papers, LG/F/45/9, Smuts to Lloyd George, 11 Jul 1917; RAFM, Henderson papers, AC71/4/4, 'Notes on Relations of Air Force with Navy and Army for Consideration by General Smuts' Committee' (n.d.).

7 See on this Brock Millman, 'A Counsel of Despair: British Strategy and War Aims 1917–18', *Journal of Contemporary History*, 36 (2001), pp. 244–50; Richard Toye, *Lloyd George and Churchill: Rivals for Greatness* (London: Macmillan, 2007), pp. 173–4.

8 P.Arch, LG/F/45/9, Smuts to Lloyd George, 24 and 31 May 1917.

9 Ibid., Smuts to Lloyd George, 6 Jun 1917.

10 Winston Churchill, *The World Crisis, 1911–1918: Volume* II (London: Odhams, 1938), p. 1170; Toye, *Lloyd George and Churchill*, pp. 178–80.

11 John Sweetman, 'The Smuts Report of 1917: Merely Political Window Dressing?', *Journal of Strategic Studies*, 4 (1981), pp. 155–6.

12  RAFM, Henderson papers, AC71/4/4, C-in-C Home Forces to Henderson, Jul 1917.

13  Raymond Fredette, *The First Battle of Britain 1917/18* (London: Cassell, 1966), pp. 89–90.

14  For the Second Report see RAFM, Trenchard papers, MFC 76/1/2, 'Committee on Air Defence and Home Defence Against Air Raids, Second Report', 17 Aug 1917.

15  TNA, AIR 8/2, 'Memorandum of the Organisation of the Air Service', 19 Jul 1917, pp. 8–9, 13.

16  Stephen Roskill (ed.), *Documents Relating to the Naval Air Service: Volume I, 1908–1918* (London: Navy Records Society, 1969), pp. 315–16, correspondence between Lord Montagu and Lord Derby, March 1916.

17  Ibid., pp. 497–9, Lord Cowdray to General Smuts, 28 Jul 1917, on 'Duties and Functions of the Air Board'. On Cowdray's role see H. A. Jones, *The War in the Air: Volume VI* (Oxford: Oxford University Press, 1937), pp. 7–8.

18  P. Arch, LG/F/8/1/8, Churchill to Lloyd George, 2 Aug 1917.

19  TNA, AIR 1/718/29/9, War Office to Trenchard, 2 Sep 1917.

20  Roskill (ed.), *Naval Air Service: Volume I*, p. 513, 'Second report of the Committee on Air Organisation and Home Defence', 17 Aug 1917.

21  W. J. Reader, *Architect of Airpower: The Life of the First Viscount Weir* (London: Collins, 1968), pp. 57–9. See too Neville Jones, *Origins of Strategic Bombing: A Study of the Development of British Air Strategic Thought and Practice up to 1918* (London: William Kimber, 1973), pp. 137–40; Sweetman, 'The Smuts Report of 1917', pp. 163–4.

22  Reader, *Architect of Airpower*, p. 63. On the 'Surplus Air Fleet' see the discussion in Cowdray's memorandum for Smuts on 28 Jul 1917 in Roskill (ed.), *Naval Air Service: Volume I*, pp. 489–90.

23  Reader, *Architect of Air Power*, pp. 60–63.

24 See the details in LHA, Brooke-Popham papers, 1/8, RAF Staff College Notes, 1924, 'Air Raids on England; Report by the Home Office on the Effect of Air Raids (9.3.22)', pp. 3–14.

25 RAFM, Henderson papers, AC71/4/4, 'Memorandum for the President of the Air Board', 11 Oct 1917, p. 3.

26 CCAC, WEIR 1/2, memorandum by Sir Henry Norman for the Air Minister, 'Long-range Bombing', 25 Mar 1918, p. 2.

27 TNA, AIR 8/2, War Cabinet 223, draft minutes, 24 Aug 1917.

28 Luck, 'The Smuts Report' in Sheffield and Gray (eds.), *Changing War*, p. 159; Reader, *Architect of Air Power*, pp. 65–6.

29 Roskill (ed.), *Naval Air Service: Volume I*, pp. 520–22, Beatty to Geddes, 22 Aug 1917.

30 Ibid., pp. 497–9, Jellicoe, 'Remarks on a Scheme of an Imperial Air Policy', 14 Aug 1917.

31 Ibid., pp. 491–2, Captain O. Swann to Director of Air Services, Admiralty, 9 Aug 1917.

32 TNA, WO 158/35, Royal Flying Corps, Summary of Operations 1917, reports for 1 May, 22 Jul, 3 Sep.

33 R. D. Layman, *Naval Aviation in the First World War: Its Impact and Influence* (London: Chatham Publishing, 1996), pp. 74–5.

34 TNA, AIR 1/718/29/9, Lord Derby to Trenchard, 2 Sep 1917.

35 Luck, 'The Smuts Report', p. 158.

36 TNA, AIR 1/718/29/9, Trenchard to Chief of the Imperial General Staff, 30 Aug 1917.

37 Ibid. 'Memorandum on Future Air Organization, Fighting Policy, and Requirements in Personnel and Materiel', 10 Oct 1917.

38 Ibid.,Trenchard to Lt.-General L. E. Kiggel, 21 Oct 1917.

39 John Laffin, *Swifter than Eagles: A Biography of Marshal of the RAF Sir John Salmond* (Edinburgh: Blackwood, 1964), p. 95.

40 TNA, AIR 8/2, memorandum by General Smuts for the War Cabinet, 18 Sep 1917.

41 Details of raids from TNA, WO 158/950, Report on Air Raids, 24 Sep–1 Nov 1917, pp. 5–11,107, 108.

42 White, *Zeppelin Nights*, pp. 215–18.

43 RAFM, Henderson papers, AC71/4/4, 'Memorandum for the President of the Air Board', 11 Oct 1917; Russell Miller, *Trenchard: Father of the Royal Air Force* (London: Weidenfeld & Nicolson, 2016), p. 181.

44 LHA, Brooke-Popham papers, 1/8, RAF Staff College Notes, 'Effect of Air Raids on Railway Traffic', pp. 2–3.

45 Ibid., 'Report by the Home Office on the Effect of Raids', 9 Mar 1922.

46 RAFM, AIR 69/2651, RAF Staff College Notes, 'The War 1914–1918', XV, 'The Independent Force'.

47 TNA, AIR 1/2085/207/5/3, Approximate results, 41st Wing RAF, 'Résumé of operations', 16/17 Oct 1917.

48 Francis Mason, *The British Bomber since 1914* (London: Putnam, 1994), pp. 67–74.

49 TNA, AIR 1/725/97/6, GHQ Report (RAF) for 1 Jan–31 Jul 1918, p. 7.

50 LHA, Brooke-Popham papers, 8/5, Air Ministry, 'Report of Air Raids on Germany, January 1–November 11 1918', Jan 1920, pp. 1–3, 64; 1/8, RAF Staff College Notes, Dec 1924, Policy Report No. 5, 'Statistics of Independent Force, Work Carried Out'.

51 TNA, AIR 8/2, minute for Trenchard, 'Supplementary Note on the Intentions of the Government in setting up a unified Air Service in 1917'.

52 TNA, MEPO 2/1622, Air Force (Constitution) Act, 1917, 29 Nov 1917, pp. 1, 2, 4.

53 Reproduced in Roskill (ed.), *Naval Air Service: Volume I*, pp. 581–3.

54 S. J. Taylor, *The Great Outsiders: Northcliffe, Rothermere, and the Daily Mail* (London: Weidenfeld & Nicolson, 1996), p. 229; Lord

Beaverbrook, *Men and Power, 1917–1918* (London: Hutchinson, 1956), pp. 217–18.

55 Miller, *Trenchard*, pp. 186–9.

56 TNA, AIR 1/718/29/9, Trenchard to the War Office, 6 Oct 1917.

57 Taylor, *The Great Outsiders*, p. 230.

58 Miller, *Trenchard*, pp. 189–90; CUL, Boyle papers, Add 9429/1B/209 (i), 'Notes by Trenchard for Major Lockhart' (n.d.), p. 3.

59 RAFM, Trenchard papers, MFC 76/1/18, Trenchard to Haig, 31 Dec 1917; Haig to Lord Derby, 10 Jan 1918.

60 Roskill (ed.), *Naval Air Service: Volume I*, pp. 670–71, Geddes to Lord Weir, 22 May 1918.

61 Ibid., p. 619, Air Ministry letter to Admiralty, 19 Jan 1918.

62 Ibid., pp. 641–2, extracts from Admiralty Weekly Orders, 19 Mar 1918.

63 RAFM, Sykes papers, AC73/35/3/4/1, letter by Lord Rothermere in the *Daily Telegraph*, 15 Apr 1918.

64 TNA, AIR 6/12, Air Council minutes, 3rd, 6th and 8th meetings, 11 Jan, 22 Jan, 29 Jan.

65 TNA, AIR 6/12, Air Council minutes 13th meeting, 16th meeting, 17th meeting, 19 Feb, 5 Mar, 8 Mar 1918.

66 TNA, TS 27/58, Air Board minute 12 Jan 1918; letter from Air Board to the secretary of the Air Council, 8 Jan 1918; Air Council to Sir John Mellor, 14 Jan 1918.

67 TNA, AIR 6/12, Air Council minutes, 2nd meeting, 13th meeting, 8 Jan, 19 Feb 1918.

68 RAFM, Sykes papers, AC73/35/3/4/1, Secretary of the Air Ministry to the Air Council, 21 Mar 1918.

69 RAFM, Trenchard papers, MFC 76/1/19, Trenchard to Rothermere, 18 Mar 1918; Rothermere to Trenchard, 19 Mar 1918; Trenchard to Rothermere, 19 Mar 1918; Miller, *Trenchard*, pp. 198–200.

70 Beaverbrook, *Men and Power*, p. 221.

71 RAFM, Trenchard papers, MFC 76/1/92, Trenchard to Salmond, 10 Feb 1918.

72 Ibid., Trenchard to Salmond, 13 Feb 1918.

73 Miller, *Trenchard*, p. 204.

74 Ibid., p. 202.

## 3. *April Fools' Day 1918*

1 RAFM, AC71/13/15, journal of Richard Peirse, 22 Mar 1918–15 Apr 1918, 65th Wing RNAS, Dunkirk.

2 Ibid, entries for 29 Mar, 3 Apr.

3 TNA, AIR 1/1679/204/118/2, Record Book No. 4 Squadron RNAS, 10 Mar 1918–20 Jan 1919; AIR 1/2085/207/5/3, 41st Wing RAF, Résumé of operations, night of 12/13 Apr 1918.

4 Peter Dye, 'The Bridge to Air Power: Aviation Engineering on the Western front 1914–1918', *Air Power Review*, 17 (2014), p. 11.

5 TNA, AIR 2/78, 'Order of the Air Council for Transferring and Attaching Officers and Men to the Air Force', 22 Mar 1918.

6 TNA, AIR 2/78, 'Royal Air Force Units at Home, Summary of Arrangements; Memorandum on the Organisation of the Royal Air Force in the United Kingdom', 21 Mar 1918.

7 TNA, AIR 2/78, 'Permanent Royal Air Force Stations, Approved by the Chief of the Air Staff', 12 Mar 1918.

8 TNA, AIR 1/1679/204/118/2, No. 4 (No. 204 RAF) Squadron Record Book, 10 Mar 1918–20 Jan 1919.

9 Stephen Roskill (ed.), *Documents Relating to the Naval Air Service: Volume I, 1908–1918* (London: Navy Records Society, 1969), pp. 670–71, 672–3, Geddes to Weir, 22 May 1918; Admiralty to the Air Ministry, 22 May 1918.

10 Ibid., pp. 684–6, Beatty to the Admiralty, 30 Jul 1918.

11 TNA, AIR 8/5, minutes of Air Members' Meeting, Air Ministry, 25 Oct 1918; CUL, Boyle papers, Add 9429/1B/132 (i), J. C. Nerney (Head AHB) to Trenchard, 11 Oct 1952.

12 TNA, AIR 2/38, 'Minutes of Inter-Departmental Conference on Transfer of Duties to the Air Ministry', 1 Feb 1918 (the War Office confirmed the agreement to supply and quarter the RAF on 6 Dec 1917).

13 Malcolm Cooper, 'Blueprint for Confusion: The Administrative Background to the Formation of the Royal Air Force, 1912–1919', *Journal of Contemporary History*, 22 (1987), pp. 448–9.

14 RAFM, B2717, transcript of diary of Air Mech. 2 Thomas Spencer 1916–1918, entry for 1 Jul 1918.

15 TNA, AIR 1/718/29/8, Cmd. 100, 'Synopsis of the British Air Effort', Apr 1919, p. 16.

16 Russell Miller, *Trenchard: Father of the Royal Air Force* (London: Weidenfeld & Nicolson, 2016), pp.202–3.

17 RAFM, Trenchard papers, MFC 76/1/19, Rothermere to Trenchard, 13 Apr 1918.

18 P. Arch, Lloyd George papers, LG/F/45/9, Smuts to Lloyd George, 13 Apr 1918.

19 Frederick Sykes, *From Many Angles: An Autobiography* (London: Harrap, 1942), p. 215.

20 Ibid., pp. 217–18.

21 Miller, *Trenchard*, p. 205; Lord Beaverbrook, *Men and Power, 1917–1918* (London: Hutchinson, 1956), pp. 378–9, Appendix IV, letter from Henderson to Rothermere; letter from Henderson to Bonar Law, 26 Apr 1918.

22 CUL, Boyle papers, Add 9429/1B/209 (i), notes by Trenchard for Major Lockhart (n.d.), p. 3.

23 S. J. Taylor, *The Great Outsiders: Northcliffe, Rothermere, and the Daily Mail* (London: Weidenfeld & Nicolson, 1996), pp. 231–2, 228–30; 'Beaverbrook, *Men and Power*, pp. 228–30.

24 John Laffin, *Swifter than Eagles: A Biography of Marshal of the RAF Sir John Salmond* (Edinburgh: Blackwood, 1964), p. 116.

25 Beaverbrook, *Men and Power*, pp. 222. 251.

26 W. J. Reader, *Architect of Air Power: The Life of the First Viscount Weir* (London: Collins, 1968), pp. 68–70.

27 TNA, AIR 6/12, Air Council minutes of meetings, 26th meeting, 28th meeting, 10 May and 23 May 1918.

28 John Slessor, *The Central Blue: Recollections and Reflections* (London: Cassell, 1956), p. 31; P. G. Hering, *Customs and Traditions of the Royal Air Force* (Aldershot: Gale and Polden, 1961), p. 214.

29 TNA, AIR 8/5, Air members' meetings, 27 May 1918, 21 Jun 1918; AIR 6/12, Air Council minutes, 28th meeting, 23 May 1918.

30 TNA, AIR 8/5, Air members' meetings, 17 Jul 1918, 4 Nov 1918.

31 TNA, AIR 6/14, Air Council minutes, 24 Mar 1919; AIR 2/223, 'Proposed Scheme for clothing other ranks RAF as from 1 July 1920'; 'Proceedings of Conference on Revision of Clothing for Other Ranks, Royal Air Force', Director of Equipment, May 1920; Hering, *Customs and Traditions*, p. 215.

32 TNA, ADM 1/2493, Director of RAF Quartermaster Services to Director of Stores, Admiralty, 11 May 1918; Secretary, Admiralty, to Secretary, Air Ministry, 31 May 1918; Admiralty minute 20 May 1918.

33 TNA, TS 27/67, minute from Sir Alfred Dennis for the Treasury Solicitor, Oct 1918.

34 TNA, ADM 1/12493, Admiralty to the Air Ministry, 12 Oct 1918, 8 Nov 1918.

35 Ibid., Air Ministry to Admiralty, 29 Jun 1920; Admiralty Board minutes, 8 Jul 1920; Admiralty to the Air Ministry, 26 Jul 1920; CUL, Boyle papers, Add 9429/1B/132 (i), J. C. Nerney (Head

AHB) to Trenchard, 11 Oct 1952, encl. letter from T. Marson to the Secretary of the Air Ministry, 18 Jun 1920.

36  TNA, 6/12, Air Council minutes, meetings of 1 Mar, 5 Mar 1918; AIR 1/106/15/9/284, memorandum by Lt. Col. Bersey, 1 Apr 1918, 'Women Employed in the Royal Air Force', pp. 1–3.

37  TNA, AIR 1/106/15/9/284, WRAF: Conditions of Service in the Immobile Branch; RAF Publication no. 14, 'Constitution and Regulations of the Women's Royal Air Force', p. 3.

38  Basil Collier, *Heavenly Adventurer: Sefton Brancker and the Dawn of British Aviation* (London: Secker & Warburg, 1959), p. 96.

39  CCAC, WEIR 2/7, Godfrey Paine (Master of Personnel RAF) to Douglas-Pennant, 9 Jul 1918.

40  TNA, PREM 1/205, Notes on the WRAF case (n.d.); Reader, *Architect of Air Power*, pp. 76–81.

41  Collier, *Heavenly Adventurer*, p. 23.

42  CCAC, WEIR 2/7, Douglas-Pennant to Churchill, 28 Feb 1919; Douglas-Pennant to Lloyd George, 2 Sep 1918.

43  Sykes, *From Many Angles*, p. 220; Miller, *Trenchard*, p. 204.

44  LHA, Brooke-Popham papers, 8/3, Army General Staff, 'Fighting in the Air', Apr 1918, p. 1; TNA, AIR 1/725/97/8, 'Policy for Operations 1918', p. 1: 'the primary task of the RAF must be to gain and maintain superiority in the air, as without such superiority the effective co-operation of aircraft with other arms is hindered . . .'

45  Ibid., pp. 1–3.

46  LHA, Brooke-Popham papers, 8/3, General Staff paper, 'Offence versus Defence in the Air', Oct 1917.

47  TNA, AIR 1/175/15/163/4, 65th Squadron Record Book, Jun 1918.

48  Sykes, *From Many Angles*, pp. 223–4; H. A. Jones, *The War in the Air: Appendices* (Oxford: Oxford University Press, 1937), p. 170.

49  TNA, AIR 1/462/15/312/121, Tiverton to Capt. Vyvyan (Air Board), 3 Sep 1917, pp. 1–13; AIR 1/460/15/312/97, memorandum

by Wing Commander Randall for Capt. Stopford, 4 Dec 1917; Tiverton to Rear-Admiral Mark Kerr, 1 Dec 1917.

50 TNA, AIR 1/460/15/312/97, DFO memorandum, 'Strategic Bombing. Objectives in Order of Importance' (n.d.).

51 TNA, AIR 1/718/29/9, 'Memorandum on Future Air Organisation, Fighting Policy, and Requirements in Personnel and Materiel', 10 Oct 1917, p. 5.

52 TNA, AIR 1/725/97/7, memorandum, 'Long Distance Bombing', 26 Nov 1917, p. 5.

53 CCAC, WEIR 1/6, 'Memorandum for the War Cabinet on Certain Lines of Main Policy involving the activities of the Air Ministry', 14 May 1918; Lord Weir, 'Memorandum of Independent Air Force Command for long-range bombing of Germany', 25 May 1918.

54 TNA, AIR 9/8, Chief of Air Staff, 'Review of Air Situation and Strategy for the information of the Imperial War Cabinet', 27 Jun 1918, pp. 2, 6.

55 RAFM, AIR 69/2651, 'The War of 1914–18', RAF Staff College Notes, 'The Independent Force'.

56 CCAC, WEIR 1/6, private memorandum, 27 Apr 1918.

57 RAFM, Trenchard papers, MFC 76/1/19, Trenchard to the War Office, 14 Apr 1918; Rothermere to Lord Derby, 14 Apr 1918. See too Miller, *Trenchard*, pp. 209–10.

58 RAFM, Trenchard papers, MFC 76/1/20, Trenchard to Weir, 5 May 1918; Weir to Trenchard, 6 May 1918; Trenchard to Weir, 8 May 1918.

59 Trenchard papers, MFC 76/1/28, Air Ministry to Trenchard, 13 May 1918; memorandum for the War Cabinet from Lord Weir, 22 May 1918.

60 Miller, *Trenchard*, p.213 (citing Trenchard's private diary).

61 RAFM, AIR 69/3, 'Despatch from Major General Sir Hugh Trenchard on the Work of the Independent Air Force', p. 1.

62 RAFM, Trenchard papers, MFC 76/1/28, memorandum by Lord Weir for the War Cabinet; 76/1/3, letter from Haig to the War Cabinet, 20 Nov 1917; LHA, Brooke-Popham papers, 8/5, Air Ministry, 'Results of Raids on Germany, January 1st–November 11th 1918'.

63 TNA, AIR 8/179, 'Interview with Lord Trenchard on the Independent Air Force', 11 Apr 1934, p. 6.

64 LHA, Brooke-Popham papers, 1/8, RAF Staff College Notes, 'Memorandum on the Bombing of Germany submitted to the Inter-Allied Aviation Committee of the Supreme War Council, 23 Jun 1918'.

65 RAFM, AIR 69/3, 'Despatch from Major General Sir Hugh Trenchard . . .', p. 4.

66 TNA, AIR 1/2085/207/5/3, 'Independent Force: Approximate Results, 9 July 1918–11 November 1918'.

67 TNA, AIR 1/460/15/312/97, Groves to Chief of the Air Staff, 11 Sep 1918.

68 LHA, Brooke-Popham papers, 1/8, RAF Staff College Notes, Memorandum No. 3, 'Notes on Night Reconnaissance and Bombing, July 1918', pp. 1, 5; Memorandum No. 5, 'Statistics of Independent Force'.

69 RAFM, AIR 69/3, lecture by Air Vice-Marshal Brooke-Popham, 'The Air Force in its Role as a Separate Service' (n.d.), p. 3.

70 TNA, AIR 1/2085, Independent Force communiqué for Air Ministry, 1 Nov 1918.

71 TNA, AIR 1/718/29/5, 'Report on Operations August 1918, Independent Air Force', 1 Sep 1918; AIR 1/2085, Independent Force Communiqués, 5/6 Jun 1918.

72 Edward Westermann, *Flak: German Anti-Aircraft Defenses, 1914–1945* (Lawrence, KA: Kansas University Press, 2001), pp. 18–27.

73 RAFM, AIR 69/3, Sq/L Drummond to Sq/L Mackay, 11 Dec 1923, reference query on IAF casualties.

74 Ibid., 'Independent Air Force, Notes by Air Vice-Marshal Brooke-Popham', pp. 5–7.

75 RAFM, Sykes papers, AC 73/35/3/5/1, minute by Chief of the Air Staff, 'Independent Bombing Command', for the Prime Minister, 1 Jun 1918.

76 RAFM, Sykes papers, AC 73/35/3/5/1, memorandum of a conversation between Lloyd George, Clemenceau and Sykes, 3 Jun 1918.

77 RAFM, AIR 69/2651, RAF Staff College Notes, 'Note from Lord Weir to M. Clemenceau', 26 Aug 1918.

78 Eric Ash, *Sir Frederick Sykes and the Air Revolution 1912–1918* (London: Frank Cass, 1999), pp. 161–3.

79 RAFM, Sykes papers, AC 73/35/3/5/1, 'Note on the Inter-Allied Bombing Force Problem', British Section, Supreme War Council, 23 Jul 1918.

80 Sykes, *From Many Angles*, pp. 232–3.

81 Laffin, *Swifter than Eagles*, p. 97.

82 CCAC, WEIR 1/5, Air Ministry, 'Synopsis of British Air Effort', p. 12.

83 Richard Overy, 'Strategic Bombardment before 1939: Doctrine, Planning, and Operations', in R. Cargill Hall (ed.), *Case Studies in Strategic Bombardment* (Washington, DC: Air Force History Program, 1998), pp. 21–2. The best account of Anglo-American thinking about strategic bombing is Tami Davis Biddle, *Rhetoric and Reality in Air Warfare: The Evolution of British and American Ideas about Strategic Bombing 1914–1945* (Princeton, NJ: Princeton University Press, 2002).

84 M. Maurer, *The U.S Air Service in World War I,* 4 vols. (Washington, DC: Office of Air Force History, 1978), Vol. ii, p. 132, 'Report by Major R. C. Bolling to Chief Signal Officer, 15 August 1917'.

85 National Archives and Records Administration, College Park, MD, RG 18/11, Division of Military Aeronautics, 'Accomplish-

ments and Program Requirements under Maj. General Wm
L. Kenly April–November 1918', 1 Jul 1919, p. 8.

86 R. D. Layman, *Naval Aviation in the First World War: Its Impact and Influence* (London: Chatham Publishing, 1996), pp. 86, 209–11.

87 TNA, AIR 9/2, 'Combined Naval Operations in the North Sea 1914/1918' (n.d.). Out of sixty-six seaplane sorties, thirty-one failed to rise from the sea.

88 TNA, AIR 9/5, note by the Chief of the Imperial General Staff, 16 Sep 1921. Modern calculations can be found in Christopher Cook and E. F. Cheesman, *The Air Defence of Britain, 1914–1918* (London: Putnam, 1984), pp. 418–19.

89 LHA, Brooke-Popham papers, 1/8, 'Statistics on German Air Raids on England. Results of German Bomb Raids'.

90 Brooke-Popham papers, 1/8, RAF Staff College Notes, 'Statistics of Independent Force, Work Carried Out', pp. 1–2.

91 RAFM, AIR 69/2651, RAF Staff College Notes, 'The War of 1914–1918', Appendix 3, 'Weight of Bombs dropped on Targets more than 85 miles from the Front Line'.

92 Peter Dye, 'The Bridge to Air Power: Aviation Engineering on the Western Front 1914–1918', *Air Power Review*, 17 (2014), p. 13; Alan Morris, *First of the Many: The Story of Independent Force, RAF* (London: Jarrolds, 1968), Appendix A.

93 Cooper, 'Blueprint for Confusion', p. 448.

94 TNA, AIR 1/2085, 'Communiqué to all Personnel of the Independent Force', 11 Nov 1918; Arnold Harvey, 'The Royal Air Force and Close Support, 1918–1940', *War in History*, 15 (2008), p. 420.

95 LHA, Brooke-Popham papers, 8/5, Air Ministry, 'Results of the Air Raids on Germany January 1st – November 11th 1918', Jan 1920, pp. 1, 3.

96 RAFM, Air 69/3, 'Despatch from Major General Sir Hugh Trenchard on the Work of the Independent Air Force', 31 Dec 1918.

97 Susan Grayzel, *At Home and Under Fire: Air Raids and Culture in Britain from the Great War to the Blitz* (Cambridge: Cambridge University Press, 2012), p. 85, citing a diary by Ethel Bilbrough, 4 Nov 1917.

98 Ash, *Sir Frederick Sykes*, p. 162.

99 Sykes, *From Many Angles*, p. 231.

100 TNA, AIR 1/725/97/7, Trenchard to Salmond, 4 Nov 1918.

101 Heinz Hanke, *Luftkrieg und Zivilbevölkerung* (Frankfurt/Main: Peter Lang, 1991), pp. 6–8.

102 Joel Hayward, 'Air Power, Ethics, and Civilian Immunity during the First World War and its Aftermath', *Global War Studies*, 7 (2010), pp. 118–22.

103 TNA, AIR 8/3, War Cabinet minutes, 16 Oct 1919.

104 Dye, 'Bridge to Air Power', pp. 12–13. See too David Jordan, 'The Genesis of Modern Air Power: The RAF in 1918' in Gary Sheffield and Peter Gray (eds.), *Changing War: The British Army, the Hundred Days Campaign, and the Birth of the Royal Air Force, 1918* (London: Bloomsbury, 2013), pp.192–203; Harvey, 'Royal Air Force Close Support', pp. 466–70.

105 LHA, Groves papers, Box 2 (a), Brig.-Gen. Geoffrey Salmond to Groves (n.d.).

## 4. 'A Very Gruelling Business': Saving the RAF

1 TNA, AIR 9/5, Note by Winston Churchill at the Colonial Office on a 'Separate Force', 24 Oct 1921, p.1.

2  LHA, Brooke-Popham papers, 9/ 5, Brooke-Popham to H.A. Jones, 6 Jun 1933; Jones to Brooke-Popham, 9 Jun 1933; Draft of speech, Royal Air Force dinner, 23 Jun 1933.

3  TNA, AIR 8/6, 'Memorandum of the Chief of the Air Staff on Air Requirements of the Empire', pp. 1–4.

4  TNA, ADM 116/1836, 'Minutes of a conference held between Admiralty and Air Ministry on Jan 2 1919', p. 8.

5  Eric Ash, *Sir Frederick Sykes and the Air Revolution 1912–1918* (London: Frank Cass, 1999), p. 176.

6  LHA, Brooke-Popham papers, 8/3, 'A Brief History of British Air Services 1910–1935', p. 10.

7  John Laffin, *Swifter than Eagles: The Biography of Marshal of the RAF Sir John Salmond* (Edinburgh: Blackwood, 1964), p. 146.

8  R. D. Layman, *Naval Aviation in the First World War: Its Impact and Influence* (London: Chatham Publishing, 1996), p. 196.

9  TNA, ADM 116/1836, Admiral Commanding Aircraft to commander-in-chief Atlantic and Home Fleets, 14 Apr 1919; AIR 6/14, Air Council minutes, 18 Mar 1919, p. 6; CUL, Boyle papers, Add 9429/1B/207-15, report of lecture by CAS to officers of the RAF, 22 Jan 1926.

10  TNA, AIR 6/14, Air Council minutes, 18 Mar 1919, p. 6; Beryl Escott, *Women in Air Force Blue: The Story of Women in the Royal Air Force from 1918 to the Present Day* (Wellingborough: Patrick Stephens, 1989), p. 295.

11  W. J. Reader, *Architect of Air Power: The Life of the First Viscount Weir* (London: Collins,1968), p. 81.

12  P. Arch, Lloyd George papers, LG/F/8/1, Churchill to Lloyd George, 7 Nov 1918; Churchill to Lloyd George, 9 Nov 1918.

13  Stephen Roskill, *Hankey: Man of Secrets: Volume II, 1919–1931* (London: Harper Collins, 1972), p. 46.

14  P. Arch, LG/F/8/1, Churchill to Lloyd George, 29 Dec 1918.

15  CCAC, CHAR 2/105/3, Churchill to Lloyd George, 10 Jan 1919.

16 CCAC, CHAR 16/1, Churchill to the Admiralty, 8 Feb 1919.

17 David Omissi, *Air Power and Colonial Control: The Royal Air Force 1919–1939* (Manchester: Manchester University Press, 1990), p. 8.

18 Winston Churchill, *Thoughts and Adventures* (London: Macmillan, 1942), pp. 153, 158, 166–7.

19 CUL, Boyle papers, Add 9429/1B/219-57, Churchill to Hilary St George Saunders, 7 Jun 1951.

20 Russell Miller, *Trenchard: Father of the Royal Air Force* (London: Weidenfeld & Nicolson, 2016), pp. 236–7.

21 CUL, Boyle papers, Add 9429/1B/207-15, report of lecture delivered by CAS to officers of the RAF, 22 Jan 1926, pp. 1–2.

22 Ibid., 1B/268 (i), Notes on chapters by Major Lockhart, 18 Jan 1954, p. 1.

23 TNA, AIR 8/5, minutes of Air Members' meeting, 17 Jul 1918.

24 TNA, AIR 6/14, Air Council minutes, 18 Mar 1919; P. G. Hering, *Customs and Traditions of the Royal Air Force* (Aldershot: Gale and Polden, 1961), p. 22; H. A. Jones, *The War in the Air: Volume* VI (Oxford: Oxford University Press, 1937), p. 25.

25 CUL, Boyle papers, Add 2429/1B/132 (v), note by Trenchard, 27 Oct 1952; Hering, *Customs and Traditions*, p. 23.

26 Henry Probert, *Bomber Harris: His Life and Times* (London: Greenhill Books, 2006), pp. 45–6.

27 LHA, Groves papers, 6/3, Groves to Secretary, Air Ministry, 7 Apr 1919; Groves to Air Ministry, 16 Apr 1919; Air Ministry, Master of Personnel, to Groves, 13 May 1919; Groves to Trenchard, Jan 1920; Trenchard to Groves, 10 Feb 1920; Air Ministry to Groves, 31 Mar 1920.

28 LHA, Brooke-Popham papers, 8/3, E. Halford Ross, 'Report of the Committee on the Preliminary Education of Candidates for Royal Air Force Commissions', 15 Mar 1919, pp. 1–3.

29 CUL, Boyle papers, Add 9429/1B/207-15, report of lecture delivered by CAS, 22 Jan 1926; John James, *The Paladins: A Social*

*History of the* RAF *up to the Outbreak of World War* II (London: Macdonald, 1990), pp. 109–11.

30 TNA, AIR 9/5, Trenchard memorandum 'on the Status of the Royal Air Force', 14 Aug 1919.

31 Miller, *Trenchard*, p. 245.

32 TNA, AIR 1/718/29/2, 'Memorandum on Why the Royal Air Force should be maintained as separate from the Navy and Army', 11 Sep 1919, pp. 1–2, 4.

33 TNA, AIR 1/718/29/7, Trenchard to Churchill, enclosing draft 'Memorandum by the Air Staff on the Reconstruction of the Royal Air Force', 22 Nov 1919.

34 TNA, AIR 1/718/29/8, memorandum by the Chief of the Air Staff, 25 Nov 1919.

35 LHA, Brooke-Popham papers, Cmd. 467, 'Royal Air Force', 11 Dec 1919.

36 Omissi, *Air Power and Colonial Control*, p. 22.

37 TNA, AIR 9/5, 'Memorandum prepared by the General Staff for the Committee of Imperial Defence', 26 May 1921.

38 TNA, AIR 9/5, 'Note by the CIGS on Mr. Balfour's Memorandum', 16 Sep 1921.

39 Ibid., 'Draft notes by the Chief of the Air Staff for the Secretary of State', Sep 1921; 'Notes by the Air Staff on the main policy Observations by the Committee on National Expenditure', Oct 1921.

40 Omissi, *Air Power and Colonial Control*, pp. 28–9.

41 TNA, AIR 8/17, Beatty to Churchill, 19 Mar 1922; Beatty to Churchill, 17 Jul 1922.

42 Ibid., Trenchard to Churchill, 'The Question of Air Personnel Working with the Navy', 24 Mar 1922; Trenchard memorandum, 19 Jul 1922; AIR 8/2, Air Staff, 'History of the Establishment of a Separate Air Force and its Relations with the other Services' (n.d.).

43  TNA, AIR 8/3, 'Note on Agreement between the First Lord of the Admiralty and the Secretary of State for Air', 26 Feb 1923; Omissi, *Air Power and Colonial Control*, pp. 31–3.

44  CCAC, TRENCHARD 4, Cabinet paper 394(24), relations between the Navy and the Royal Air Force: note by the Lord Chancellor, 1 Jul 1924; Trenchard and Keyes to Lord Haldane, 4 Jul 1924, encl. Cmd 1938 on air–naval cooperation.

45  TNA, AIR 8/6, 'Memorandum by the Chief of the Air Staff', 9 Dec 1918, p. 1.

46  Jafna Cox, 'A Splendid Training Ground: The Importance to the Royal Air Force of its Role in Iraq, 1919–32', *Journal of Imperial and Commonwealth History*, 13 (1984–5), pp. 169–76.

47  Omissi, *Air Power and Colonial Control*, pp. 10–15, 25–6, 31–6. See too Sebastian Ritchie, *The RAF, Small Wars and Insurgencies in the Middle East, 1919–1939* (Northolt: Air Historical Branch, 2011), esp. pp. 78–83.

48  TNA, AIR 9/5, Notes by the Air Staff on the main policy observations by Committee on National Expenditure, Oct 1921, p. 3.

49  TNA, ADM 116/1836, memorandum by Admiral R. Wemyss for the War Cabinet, 'Postwar Functions of the Air Ministry and Postwar Strength of the Royal Air Force', 7 Jan 1919, p. 2.

50  John Laffin, *Swifter than Eagles: A biography of Marshal of the Royal Air Force Sir John Salmond* (Edinburgh: Blackwood, 1964), pp. 150, 156; David Richardson, 'The Royal Air Force and the Irish War of Independence', *Air Power Review*, 19 (2016), pp. 15–16.

51  TNA, AIR 9/2, Air Staff memorandum, 'The Big Ship Controversy from the Air Point of View', 20 Jan 1921, pp. 5, 8–9.

52  TNA, AIR 9/2, Air Staff memorandum, 'Is the Fleet Air Arm part of the Royal Air Force?', 26 May 1926, p. 2; Air 8/17, Trenchard to Churchill, 24 Mar 1922.

53  Omissi, *Air Power and Colonial Control*, p. 31; Miller, *Trenchard*, pp. 274–5.

54 CUL, Boyle papers, Add 9429 1B/95 (i), Wing Commander T. Marson to Trenchard, 8 Jul 1954.

55 CCAC, TRENCHARD 1, Churchill to Chamberlain, 11 Mar 1922; TNA, AIR 8/2, Extract from Hansard, 16 Mar 1922, p. 5.

56 Omissi, *Air Power and Colonial Control*, pp. 33–4.

57 CUL, Boyle papers, Add 9429/1B/68, Trenchard to Lord Hankey (Secretary to the Cabinet in 1923), 8 Feb 1952; 1B/283 (ii), notes by Sir Christopher Bullock on his years at the Air Ministry (n.d.), p. 4.

58 TNA, AIR 9/5, Statement by the prime minister, 25 Feb 1926; AIR 8/2, Sir Christopher Bullock, (PPS to Hoare), 'Supplementary note on the Intentions of the Government in setting up a unified Air Service in 1917', 11 Feb 1926.

59 CUL, Boyle papers, Add 9429/1B/333, John Steel to Major Lockhart, 24 Mar 1955.

60 CCAC, TRENCHARD 1, Churchill to Chamberlain, 11 Mar 1922.

61 Richardson, 'The Royal Air Force and the Irish War of Independence', p. 12.

62 Omissi, *Air Power and Colonial Control*, p. 35.

63 Cox, 'A Splendid Training Ground', p. 175.

64 CUL, Boyle papers, Add 9429/1B/219, Churchill to Hilary St George Saunders, 7 Jun 1951.

65 Brett Holman, 'World Police for World Peace: British Internationalism and the Threat of a Knock-out Blow from the Air, 1919–1945', *War in History*, 17 (2010), pp. 314–7.

66 Michele Haapamaki, *The Coming of the Aerial War: Culture and Fear of Airborne Attack in Inter-War Britain* (London: I. B. Tauris, 2014), pp. 40–41.

67 John Ferris, 'The Theory of a "French Air Menace": Anglo-French Relations and the British Home Defence Air Force

Programme of 1921–25', *Journal of Strategic Studies*, 10 (1987), pp. 65–7.

68 Ibid., pp. 70–73.

69 TNA, AIR 8/6, 'Note by the CAS on a Revised Scheme for the Provision of a Home Defence Force', Jun 1922, p. 1.

70 Cox, 'A Splendid Training Ground', pp. 165–6; Ferris, 'The Theory of a "French Air Menace"', pp. 70–72, 74–7.

71 CCAC, TRENCHARD 1, Trenchard to Churchill, 25 Apr 1919, encl. 'Post War Air Force'.

72 TNA, AIR 2/1830, Revision of 1936 Manual of Combined Operations, 1938, para. 28.

73 TNA, AIR 16/108, 'Air Staff Specification A 7/39', Mar. 1939; 'Minutes of a Meeting of Operational Requirements Committee to Consider Army Cooperation Aeroplane', 29 Mar 1939.

74 TNA, AIR 14/181, Commander, Advanced Air Striking Force to Bomber Command HQ, 5 Mar 1940. Slessor comment in Peter Smith, *Impact: The Dive Bomber Pilots Speak* (London: William Kimber, 1981), p. 34.

75 See for example TNA, AIR 9/99, HQ Bomber Command to Air Ministry (Plans), Dec 1939; 'Note, The Attack of Air Force on the Ground', 9 May 1940; Plans (Ops), 'Attack of German Air Force on the Ground', 6 Sep 1939.

76 TNA, AIR 9/8, Speech by the Chief of the Air Staff to the War Office Staff Exercise, Buxton, 9–13 Apr 1923, p. 3.

77 RAFM, AIR 69/3, speech by Brooke-Popham, 'The Air Force in its role as a Separate Service' (n.d.), p. 9.

78 TNA, AIR 9/8, 'Note upon the memorandum of the Chief of the Naval Staff, Paper no. COS 156', p. 3.

79 Neville Parton, 'The Development of Early Royal Air Force Doctrine', *Journal of Military History*, 72 (2008), p. 1167.

80 TNA, AIR 8/244, Air Staff memorandum, 'The Role of the Air Force in National Defence', 5 Jul 1938.

81 TNA, AIR 16/261, Dowding to Newall, 24 Feb 1939.

82 CUL, Boyle papers, Add. 9429/1B/110 (i), Air Ministry pamphlet 317, John Slessor, 'Place of the Bomber in British Strategy', 31 Dec 1952.

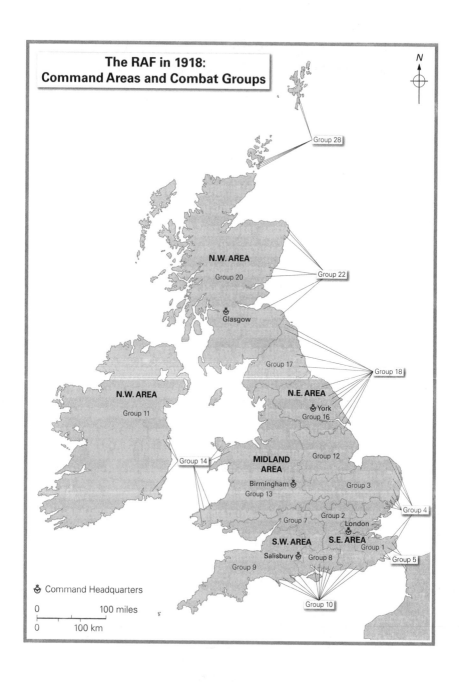

The RAF in 1918:
Command Areas and Combat Groups

N

Group 28

N.W. AREA

Group 20

Glasgow

Group 22

Group 17

Group 18

N.W. AREA

Group 11

N.E. AREA

York
Group 16

Group 14

MIDLAND
AREA

Group 12

Birmingham
Group 13

Group 3

Group 4

Group 2

Group 7

London

S.W. AREA

S.E. AREA

Group 1

Salisbury

Group 8

Group 9

Group 5

Group 10

♆ Command Headquarters

0          100 miles

0          100 km

# COMMENTARY ON PLATE SECTION

1. A carpenters' repair shop for the Royal Flying Corps. Their skills were essential to keeping the vulnerable wooden aircraft flying.

2. Major Frederick Sykes (*centre*), later chief-of-staff of the fledgling RAF, with the administrative staff of the RFC shortly before the outbreak of war. Trenchard thought he was 'a hard worker and had some brains', but the two were bitter rivals.

3. An RFC observer of the 16th Wing Photographic Section holding his camera. In the early years of air power, reconnaissance was an essential function.

4. Liberal Prime Minister Herbert Asquith (*centre, in dark civilian clothing*) watching a returning flight of aircraft land at RFC headquarters at Frevillers. To the right, with shooting stick, is General Hugh Trenchard, commander of the RFC, whose negative view of politicians seems captured in the image.

5. Hoisting an RNAS seaplane on to the sea for its flight. In 47 per cent of cases in North Sea operations the seaplanes failed to take off from the choppy surface.

6. The view from the Hotel Cecil of temporary accommodation built in the Victoria Embankment Gardens to house part of the Ministry of Munitions. The Hotel housed the Air Board and later the Air Ministry, but it developed a wartime reputation for intrigue and incompetence.

7. An aerial photograph taken by German raiders of the bombs falling on London on 7 July 1917. The raid finally triggered a government response that ended with the founding of the RAF. St Paul's Cathedral is clearly visible towards the right of the image.

8. Jan Smuts (*right*) and British Foreign Secretary Arthur Balfour after attending an Allied conference in Paris, 27 July 1917. Smuts was invited by David Lloyd George two weeks before to report on air defence and the future of British air power.

9. RFC cadets in November 1917 share a dinner in the Great Hall of Christ Church, Oxford, where they were posted for officer training. Many air officers shared a background from British public schools and the ancient universities.

10. King George V was an enthusiastic supporter of the decision to create a separate air force. Here he takes leave of Major-General John Salmond (*left*), commander of the RFC after Trenchard departed for the job of chief-of-staff.

11. An RAF chaplain leads a procession of men from No. 3 Squadron, Australian Flying Corps, carrying the coffin of Manfred von Richthofen, the legendary German air ace, to the cemetery at Bertangles. He was the most prominent early victim of the renamed RAF when his aircraft was shot down on 21 April 1918.

12. RAF mechanics prepare drawings of German aircraft for gunnery practice in 1918. By the end of the war, fighter offensives against enemy aircraft had come to replace reconnaissance as the principal activity of the air force.

13. Major John Simon (a later Chancellor of the Exchequer) inspecting one of the new heavy bombers, the Handley-Page O/400, at Ligescourt in August 1918. The aircraft was poised to become the mainstay of the independent bombing campaign.

14. American airmen are instructed at the British Aerial Gunnery School on how to hit a rapidly moving target. American participation in the air war after 1917 took time to develop and relied heavily on British and French assistance.

15. The RAF College at Cranwell, shortly after its completion in 1922. Trenchard wanted to attract 'the intelligent class' into the air force, and cadets had to meet stringent standards.

16. Winston Churchill, the Air Minister, and Trenchard at the first Hendon air pageant in 1920. The two men cemented a relationship that saw Churchill defend the independence of the RAF against attacks by the army and navy.

17. A row of Sopwith Snipe aircraft lined up next to an ambulance at Beckendorf, near Cologne, in March 1919. The Allied occupation of western Germany was one way of reinforcing the eventual peace settlement.

18. Armstrong-Whitworth Siskin aircraft of No. 29 Squadron, RAF, lined up at the Hendon Air Show in 1929. The RAF remained committed to biplane designs under Trenchard's leadership, when faster monoplanes were already in development.

19. A flight of Fairey Swordfish Mark I biplanes flying from RAF Gosport over the Solent Estuary on the English south coast. Naval aviation became the poor relation as the RAF developed, though in this case the robust Swordfish had notable success in the first years of the war despite its slow speed and ungainly appearance.

# INDEX

# RAF